"Being able to tell compelling stories is a key to success in many areas of life: business, friendship, your career, your creative life. Doug O'Brien has made storytelling accessible even for those who don't consider themselves storytellers. And for those of you who are already storytellers, this book can upgrade your story skills."

–Bill O'Hanlon, author of 40 books, including the Oprah-featured *Do One Thing Different*

"This book is jam-packed with the essentials. Doug O'Brien shows how everyone from Moses to Maya Angelou made a difference with stories. If you want to learn about leadership, the arts, or just being fun at parties, *The User's Guide to Storytelling* is a great place to start."

–Kevin Allison, host and creator of the hit true storytelling podcast and live show RISK!

"Doug O'Brien has given us a miraculously comprehensive and delightfully effervescent guide into the wonderful world of storytelling. At once practical and informative, *The User's Guide to Storytelling* is a terrific tool for any aspiring teller, and a 'must-have' for any library."

–David Gonzalez, storyteller, musician, poet, actor, and writer

"Doug has crafted an incredible reference book; concise, entertaining, and a fun read!"

–Seth Barrish, director of five of Mike Birbiglia's one-man shows, co-artistic director of The Barrow Group in New York City

The User's Guide to Storytelling

by Doug O'Brien

"You hang around, baby,
With Jean and Joan and a-who knows who"
—Santana

This book is dedicated to two inspirational wild hares...
my cousin Joan Robinson, who amazed me by being the
first person I ever met who did storytelling as an art form,
and my wife Jean E. Taylor, who kickstarted this project when
she gave me a blank book for Christmas one year she entitled
"Everybody Has a Story."

This book is how I filled those pages.

TABLE OF CONTENTS

Moroccan Storyteller, by Hermann Knottnerus-Meyer, 1926

Foreword
by Matthew Dicks

Here's the tricky thing about storytelling:

We all do it. We do it every day. We arrive home from work and tell stories about our day to partners, parents, spouses, and children. We return from vacation and share our favorite and least favorite moments with friends and neighbors. We encounter a surly cashier, a raging toddler, or a hilarious police officer and can't wait to tell others about our encounters.

And because we tell 99% of our stories to people who like and love us, we receive positive feedback for the stories we tell, even when our actual ability to tell a story is not good.

When it comes to storytelling, most people tell poorly crafted stories to adoring audiences, and they receive smiles and love in return.

This is why the world is chock full of truly remarkable stories told poorly. So what is a person to do?

One choice is to continue to tell stories poorly, which is fine. As long as your loved ones continue to love you, you can probably get away with bad storytelling. You won't become known as the great storyteller of your friend group, and you might never captivate your family at Thanksgiving with your tales of hijinks and mishaps. Still, you probably won't offend anyone, either.

You'll be average. Ordinary. Just like everyone else.

Also, you probably won't be able to rely on storytelling to get a new job, pitch a product, convince someone to go on a date with you, pass along your family history, or sell your idea.

You'll need someone else for that.

But if you're willing to be an average storyteller with interesting things to say told poorly, onward, I say. Continue to plod through life, entertaining loved ones and boring strangers.

But if you want to become a more entertaining, engaging storyteller, I have some excellent news for you:

It's not hard to do. Storytelling is a craft that can be learned, and it has nothing to do with your proficiency with the language, the size of your vocabulary, your facility with grammar, your skill as a writer, or the tone of your voice. Great storytelling is simply a matter of good decision-making. Great storytellers think before they speak and make effective choices about what to say, when to say it, how to say it, and what should be left out.

Most people don't make decisions when telling a story. They say the first thing that comes to their mind. Great storytellers make decisions, and those decisions are strategic.

But that's it. Learn to make the kinds of decisions that novelists, screenwriters, playwrights, speechwriters, columnists, and poets make, and your stories will instantly become more entertaining and engaging.

This means that people for whom English is their second, third, or fourth language can tell great stories. This means that people ages eight and eighty can tell a great story. This means someone who has not written a sentence in a quarter century can tell a great story. This means you need not be involved in a high-speed chase, a disastrous first date, or a near-death experience to tell a great story. Just make good decisions. Pile up enough of them, and you have yourself a great story.

How do you learn to make these good decisions? You learn from the best.

The good news is that in today's world, storytellers and students of storytelling like Doug O'Brien have unlocked the secrets to telling great stories, revealing the decisions that great storytellers make in order to entertain and engage audiences.

Physicists require years of study in order to become proficient in their craft. Athletes require a certain degree of innate athleticism in order to achieve greatness. Musicians must rehearse for countless hours to perform professionally.

Magicians never reveal their secrets. They are awful people.

But storytelling? You can start today, and you can become better today. You need not study for years in order to tell a great story. Storytelling does not require any hereditary trait. You don't need years of practice in order to achieve excellence.

Best of all, unlike magicians, storytellers reveal their secrets. We reveal them every day, in the stories we tell, the novels we write, the films we make, the plays we direct, the music we compose, the television shows we produce, and more. Storytelling is all around you. Simply pay attention and learn. Then there are people like Doug O'Brien who are pulling back the curtain and letting you in on the secrets, offering you a short, clearer, quicker path to success.

Congratulations on getting started on your storytelling journey. I promise that it will be one filled with internal growth and external rewards.

As Angelica Schuyler says to Alexander Hamilton in storyteller Lin-Manuel Miranda's Broadway show, *Hamilton*, "I'm about to change your life."

Well, in this particular case, Doug O'Brien is doing most of the work.

Proceed, faithful reader. We need more storytelling and better storytelling in this world. We need a more entertaining, engaging world.

We need more storytellers like the one you are about to become.

Matthew Dicks is an internationally bestselling author, playwright, columnist, and teacher. He is a fifty-three time Moth StorySLAM champion, and a seven time Moth GrandSLAM champion.

Part I
EXPLORING Storytelling and Storytellers

Why Storytelling?

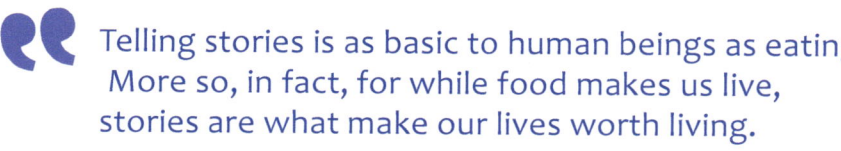 Telling stories is as basic to human beings as eating. More so, in fact, for while food makes us live, stories are what make our lives worth living.

—*On Stories,* Richard Kearney

Because . . .

In today's modern world, with the internet, texting, and streaming movies, the idea of a storyteller can seem kind of quaint and old fashioned. *Au contraire,* my friend! The power of a good story told well is arguably more important than ever, because it is so easy for your message to be drowned in that deluge of information. A good story stands out like a life preserver tossed to a floundering man. You can grab onto it and hold it tight. Stories help us connect with our audiences in a way that charts, graphs, statistics, and bullet points cannot. They help us make our speeches memorable and our messages stick.

That being said, let us pause for a moment in our excitement about stories and mention this little proviso: in this book I'm not talking so much about the "news report" type of story–the kind of story where you simply report the facts about something that happened (those types of stories often meet the same fate of most news reports and are forgotten the next day)–I'm talking about the kind of plot–driven story that keeps the audience in the palm of the storyteller's hand.

Of course, even fact-based news reports can be made more compelling to the listener (which is exactly why news organizations employ writers). This book will help you make even that kind of story better, but what I'm really talking about here are the types of stories that stick with the listener for a long, long time.

A good story "sticks"

And stick they will. Think about it. If I were to say to you, "don't be like the hare in 'The Tortoise and the Hare,'" you'd know exactly what I'm talking about. And that story was written over 2,500 years ago!

Why is storytelling so powerful? Science is proving that something organic happens in our brains when we are being told a story. Not only are the language processing parts in our brain activated, but many other parts are too. If someone tells us about how delicious certain foods were, our sensory cortex lights up. If it's about motion, our motor cortex gets active. As we listen to or watch the story, the story comes alive in our minds as if we were actually experiencing the events the storyteller is telling us.

On the other hand, if we listen to a lecture with just facts and figures and a PowerPoint presentation with endless slides, it basically hits our language processing parts of the brain, where we decode words into meaning, and that's it. Nothing else happens.

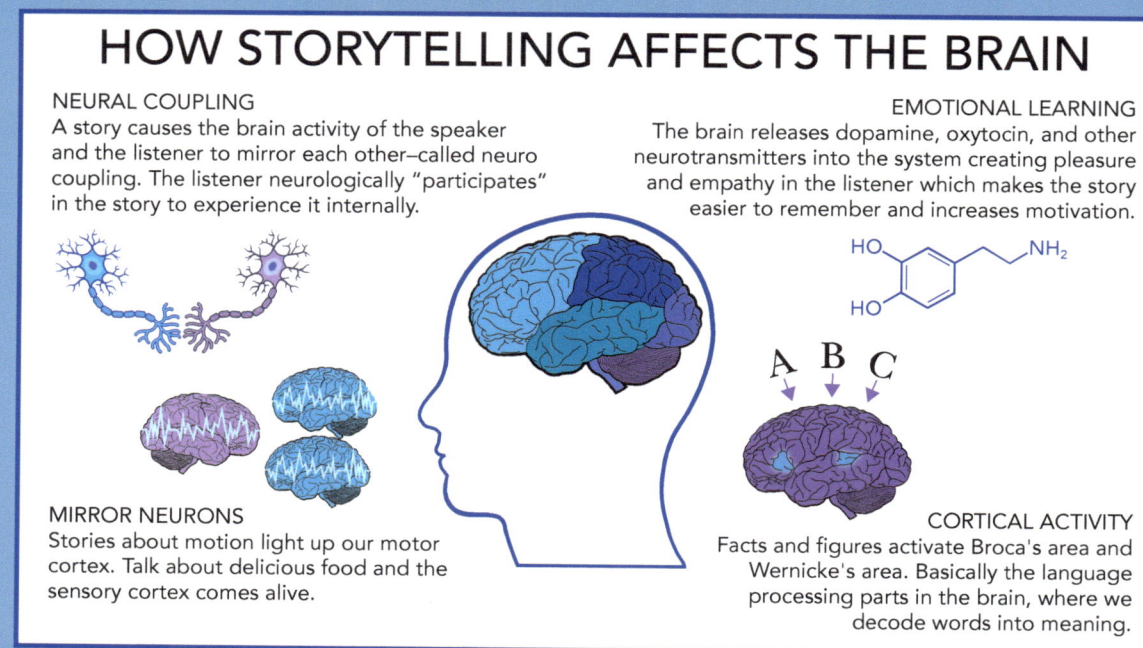

HOW STORYTELLING AFFECTS THE BRAIN

NEURAL COUPLING
A story causes the brain activity of the speaker and the listener to mirror each other—called neuro coupling. The listener neurologically "participates" in the story to experience it internally.

EMOTIONAL LEARNING
The brain releases dopamine, oxytocin, and other neurotransmitters into the system creating pleasure and empathy in the listener which makes the story easier to remember and increases motivation.

MIRROR NEURONS
Stories about motion light up our motor cortex. Talk about delicious food and the sensory cortex comes alive.

CORTICAL ACTIVITY
Facts and figures activate Broca's area and Wernicke's area. Basically the language processing parts in the brain, where we decode words into meaning.

Evolution has wired our brains for storytelling – so use it.

As you are most likely aware, stories have been with us since the dawn of humanity. Storytellers have been important and revered figures in all cultures throughout history, playing vital roles in their communities. Why? Because stories are how we've learned important lessons about life. Stories are how our brains think. Even today we think in narratives all day long, no matter if it is about buying groceries, going to work, or what our spouse is doing at home. We make up stories in our heads for every action and conversation.

Have you ever had the experience of hearing someone tell you a story and then a week later you find yourself expressing that same story to someone else as if it were your idea? This is a natural phenomenon—and one of the most powerful ways of getting people on board with your ideas. According to Uri Hasson, PhD, of the Princeton Neuroscience Institute, a story is the only way to activate parts of the brain so that a listener turns the story into their own idea and experience.

We also use stories to speculate about things that have not yet happened and to imagine what the possible results might be. Like imagining what might happen if we won the lottery or if we were to get caught cheating on our taxes. What would happen if we saw a ghost? Stories help us plan for contingencies and shape our lives.

Stories can help us answer the bigger questions of life as well. Why am I here? What happens when we die? Stories always have a beginning, middle and an end, and that can be a very comforting thing for us as we strive to write the stories of our own lives.

And, of course, stories bring us together as people. With stories we can walk in the shoes of a person from the 12th century and feel a real sense of compassion and empathy for their situation. By hearing their story we can truly appreciate the challenges of a person of another race or creed across the world from us or from right across the street. By sharing the human condition through stories, we are better able to live together as better people.

The Storyteller's Place in History

 Tell me the facts and I'll learn. Tell me the truth and I'll believe. But tell me a story and it will live in my heart forever.

—Native American Proverb

Previous: The Grandfather Tells a Story, by Albert Anker, 1884

Cave Paintings (Early Story Boarding)

The earliest form of recorded storytelling that has been discovered is from the Lascaux Caves in the Pyrenees Mountains in southern France. Discovered in 1940 by a group of French children, a series of cave paintings that date back to sometime between 15,000 and 13,000 BC depict a variety of animals and one image of a human being. When closely examined, this mural of sorts actually follows a very simplistic series of events. It tells of rituals performed and hunting practices. It tells a story.

Moreover, these cave paintings may have actually been early man's MOVIES. Moving pictures, aka movies, are actually a series of still pictures shown in a fast enough sequence that it fools the eye and we *think* it's a moving image. Well, remember, these images were viewed by the original artists and their audience by the light of a grease lamp. That flickering flame in the cave may have conjured impressions of motion like a strobe light in a dark club. In low light, human vision degrades, and that can lead to the perception of movement even when all is still, says Susana Martinez-Conde, the director of the Laboratory of Visual Neuroscience at the Barrow Neurological Institute in Phoenix, Arizona. The trick may occur at two levels; one when the eye processes a dimly lit scene, and the second when the brain makes sense of that limited, flickering information. The end result for early humans who viewed cave paintings by firelight might have been that a deer with multiple heads appeared to be a single, animated beast.

Australian Aboriginal Storytelling

Since the beginning of time, stories from what the Aborigines call "Dreamtime," (Actually, they don't call it that because they speak a different language. It's the English speakers who call it that because we don't have a better word for it. In point of fact, aboriginal spirituality does not consider the "Dreamtime" as a time in the past, or really as a time at all because "time" refers to past, present and future but the "Dreamtime" is none of these. The "Dreamtime" is there with them right now, and is not a long way away. I hope that clears things up.) played a vital role in Australian Aboriginal culture, one of the world's oldest cultures.

There are or have been more than 500 different aboriginal communities, each with their own language, so anything we write here is a generalization. Members of a given community would sit under the stars at night around the campfire—following their evening meal—and listen to storytellers recount stories from the Dreamtime, or they would hear of recent events important to the people. They had no written language, so their culture was an oral one. The storyteller's role was not just to entertain but also to preserve their culture, while educating the growing generation of children and young adults in the history, traditional values, and lore of their people.

A storyteller might tell stories of how the figures of

animals and people they saw amongst the stars above them came to live in the sky. Through stories they identified important stars that helped them navigate their way around the country, helping them to survive when in unfamiliar territory. Some were space stories that explained the arrival of showers of meteorites from outer space.

Through stories the people learned the habits of all living creatures—animals, birds, fish, insects, and plants—which explained the creatures' behavior in certain seasons and would help them to hunt successfully. Through stories they learned which berries and fruits were safe to eat, and when they were ripe for harvesting.

Often the "aunties" (older women) took the girls who were approaching woman-hood aside and told secret women's stories preparing them for their roles as wives and mothers—stories that men could not be told. Storytelling was also used by the men in sacred initiation ceremonies where "secret" information was passed on to young boys approaching manhood. Women were not allowed to know these stories.

When telling the children stories, the story-teller gave no explanation of the meaning of them. All the stories they told carried hidden knowledge that reached down to a much deeper level of understanding.

The Griot

A Griot is a West African historian, story-teller, praise singer, poet and, usually, musician. The griot is a repository of oral tradition and is often seen as a societal leader due to his traditional position as an advisor to royal personages. As a result of the former of these two functions, he is sometimes also called a bard. While the spoken word remains the key tool of a griot, he or she also retains a close bond with music. According to Paul Oliver in his book *Savannah Syncopators*, "Though the griot has to know many traditional songs without error, he or she must also have the ability to extemporize on current events, chance incidents and the passing scene. His wit can be devastating and his knowledge of local history formidable." Although they are popularly known as "praise singers," griots may use their vocal expertise for gossip, satire, or political comment.

Anyone could tell a story, but there is only one official griot per village. If a village tried to steal or entice away a griot from another village, war could break out. The griots did not work in the fields. Their job was to tell stories. Griots frequently compare their work to an ancient baobab tree or a library – a living, speaking testimony to a society's history wwithout which the knowledge of what happened would be forever lost.

Aesop (c. 620–564 BC)

Perhaps it's fitting, since we're making the point that stories stick in our collective minds better than simple facts and figures do, that we know more of Aesop's stories than we know about Aesop. We know that his stories were first written down around 300 BC, but we're not sure if he wrote—as in *created*—the stories, told the stories or simply collected stories that have come down through history as Aesop's fables.

There's just not much about Aesop that can be definitively proven. We know he lived in ancient Greece, but we're not even sure he was Greek. Some histories depict Aesop as a black African from Ethiopia. The fact that there is no reliable depiction of the man did not stop later authors and painters from concocting some. In the 1st or 2nd century AD a highly fictional biography now commonly called *The Aesop Romance* first appeared. In this account he is described as a strikingly ugly slave who by his cleverness acquires freedom and becomes an advisor to kings and city-states, but there is no proof that anything in that account has any connection to reality.

Animals are the main characters in his fables, which show how a problem is solved and a moral or lesson is learned. Aesop's stories include "The Boy Who Cried Wolf" and "The Tortoise and the Hare" and are fantastic examples of how a good story captures the imagination and sticks with us for a long time.

Homer

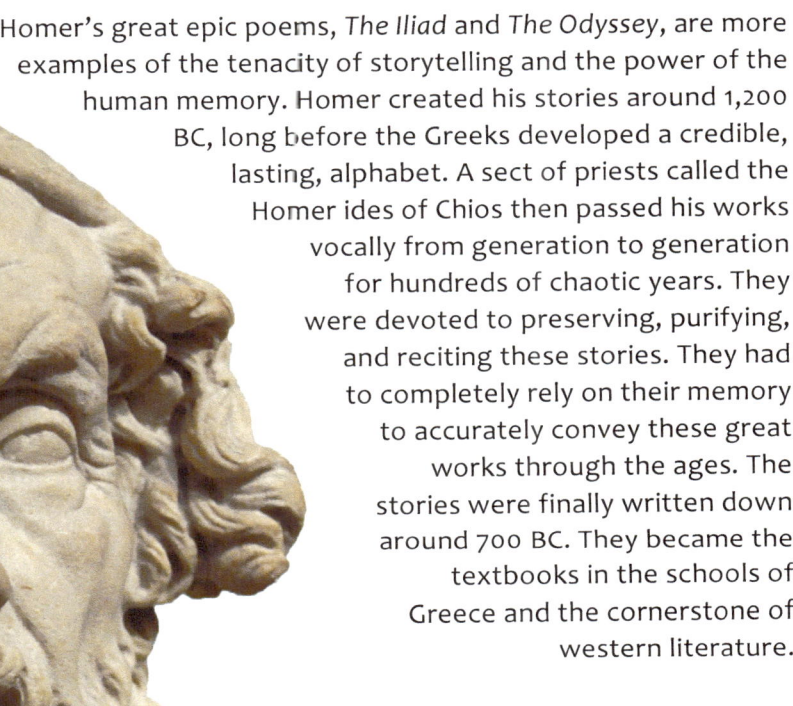

Homer's great epic poems, *The Iliad* and *The Odyssey*, are more examples of the tenacity of storytelling and the power of the human memory. Homer created his stories around 1,200 BC, long before the Greeks developed a credible, lasting, alphabet. A sect of priests called the Homer ides of Chios then passed his works vocally from generation to generation for hundreds of chaotic years. They were devoted to preserving, purifying, and reciting these stories. They had to completely rely on their memory to accurately convey these great works through the ages. The stories were finally written down around 700 BC. They became the textbooks in the schools of Greece and the cornerstone of western literature.

Like Aesop, little is known about the life of Homer. Historians place his birth sometime around 750 BC and conjecture that he was born and resided in or near Chios. However, seven cities claim to have been his birthplace, so we're not really certain. Some scholars even argue that several different authors may have written his poems.

What is undeniable is that the works of Homer proved to be tremendously influential not merely for the poets of ancient times, but also for the later epic poets of Western literature.

Moses (1391–1271 BC)

Moses was known as a great storyteller. He was very tall and had a great booming voice. We know this because why else would they have cast Charlton Heston to play him in the movie?

The first five books of the Bible's Old Testament are known as the *Books of Moses.* They are also called the *Pentateuch* and include such favorites as *Genesis, Exodus, Leviticus, Numbers,* and *Deuteronomy.* The word "Pentateuch" comes from the Greek word "penta" for five and "teuchos" meaning scrolls or volumes. (So we know for sure Moses didn't call them that since he didn't speak Greek.) Sometimes it is referred to as the Torah or The Law, and sometimes it is referred to as "The Law of Moses." Some Bible scholars believe that Moses wrote these five books and other Bible scholars disagree. We'll leave that up to them to figure out. For our purposes let's just agree that he must have been a pretty good storyteller and deserves a mention in our lineup of historically memorable storytellers. Oh, and the stories themselves were pretty memorable as well, obviously. You probably know some of them. Many of them have been made into movies over the years and have done very well at the box office.

Jesus of Nazareth (0-33)

Jesus of Nazareth was born, well, in Nazareth a long time ago. Actually—interesting fact—if you take whatever the year part is of today's date is, that's how many years ago he was born. And that will remain true no matter when you read this! Crazy huh?

If you need us to explain his life story it'd probably be easier if you just Google it.

Anyway, he was known as an awesome storyteller. Some of his stories are like Aesop's fables in that #1, they contain moral guidance and #2, many people will know the whole story and its moral just if you say the title of the story. Like "The Good Samaritan," or "The Prodigal Son."

However, unlike Aesop, Jesus's stories were not about animals, they were about people. Jesus called his stories "parables" but that's really kind of a branding thing. A parable is a type of analogy or metaphor. A parable is a succinct story, in prose or verse, which illustrates one or more moral lessons or principles. It differs from a fable in that fables employ animals, plants, inanimate objects, or forces of nature as characters, whereas parables have human characters.

Some biblical scholars apply the term "parable" only to the parables of Jesus; others disagree and apply the term to any story that meets the criteria even if someone other that Jesus told it.

It has been said that Jesus was such a good storyteller that after he got to the punch line, people were known to say things like, "Jesus! Are you serious?" In fact, similar expressions are still used to this day in several parts of the world.

Scheherazade (1,000+ Arabian Nights)

According to legend—at least we hope it's a legend—a Persian king one day discovered that his first wife had been unfaithful to him. He didn't like that. So he resolved to marry a new virgin each day and to behead the previous day's wife, so that she would have no chance to be unfaithful to him. He had been working his way through ancient Persia's supply of virgins, killing many such women by the time he was introduced to Scheherazade, the vizier's daughter.

On her first night in the King's chambers, the king lay awake and listened with awe as Scheherazade began to tell a story. The night passed by, and Scheherazade stopped in the middle of the story. The king asked her to finish, but Scheherazade said there was no time, as dawn was breaking. So, the king spared her life for one day to finish the story the next night. The next night, Scheherazade finished the story and then began a second, even more exciting tale, which she again stopped halfway through at dawn. Again, the king spared her life for one more day so she could finish the second story.

And so the King kept Scheherazade alive day by day, as he eagerly anticipated the finishing of the previous night's story. At the end of 1,001 nights, and 1,000 stories, Scheherazade told the king that she had no more tales to tell him. During these 1,001 nights, the king had fallen in love with Scheherazade. He spared her life; made her his queen and her stories were recorded for the entire world to read. They include "Ali Baba and the Forty Thieves," "Sinbad the Sailor," and "Aladdin and the Magic Lamp."

Charles Perrault (Perrault's Fairy Tales)

Charles Perrault was born in Paris in 1628. After retiring from the legal profession he began to take popular folk tales and change them into children's fairy tales with morals. He was one of the first French authors to write especially for children. His most famous fairy tales are "Sleeping Beauty," "Little Red Riding Hood," "Tom Thumb," and "Puss in Boots."

Some readers may be shocked to discover that Perrault's original tales were far more grisly than today's versions. His version of Little Red Riding Hood, for example, made it more explicitly obvious that the 'wolf' is a man intent on preying on young girls who wander alone in the woods.

"From this story one learns that children, especially young lasses, pretty, courteous and well-bred, do very wrong to listen to strangers, And it is not an unheard thing if the Wolf is thereby provided with his dinner," he wrote.

"I say Wolf, for all wolves are not of the same sort; there is one kind with an amenable disposition— neither noisy, nor hateful, nor angry, but tame, obliging and gentle, following the young maids in the streets, even into their homes. Alas! Who does not know that these gentle wolves are of all such creatures the most dangerous!"

The version of "Sleeping Beauty" we know now is a combination of a tale by Perrault (which in turn was based on older stories dating back to the 14th century) and the Grimm Brothers' "Briar Rose," which was an oral version of Perrault's.

Jacob and Wilhelm Grimm (Grimm's Fairy Tales)

Jacob and Wilhelm Grimm were born in Germany to a prosperous family in 1785 and 1786, respectively. Unfortunately for them—but good for us—the family didn't stay prosperous for long. In 1796 their father died, and the Grimms no longer had any money. With great difficulty and determination, relying heavily on each other and receiving modest financial assistance from relatives, the brothers managed to complete their schooling and attend university. The Brothers Grimm then went on to pursue law degrees at the University of Marburg.

In what may be the first documented case of bullying, the brothers were treated as inferiors at law school. In response to their poor treatment, they hungered for recognition and worked harder than ever. Their interest in history and philology (the study of language in written historical sources) led them to medieval German literature and village oral folklore.

Despite the fact that their names are associated with *Snow White* and *Rapunzel*, the brothers didn't actually write any of those stories. In fact, the stories existed long before the two men were born. The fairy tales were part of a rich oral tradition passed down from generation to generation. This tradition began to falter as industrialization took root. Fortunately, scholars like Jacob and Wilhelm began a quest to save the stories from extinction.

They interviewed relatives and friends; collecting whatever tales they could, sometimes embellishing them (although they insisted they did not). In 1812 the brothers published their story collection under the name *Children's and Household Tales.* The table of contents reads like an A-list of fairy-tale celebrities: Cinderella, Sleeping Beauty, Snow White, Little Red Riding Hood, Rapunzel, Rumpelstiltskin, Hansel and Gretel, the Frog King and more.

It was the brothers' early preference for writing down the exact way that stories were told that made them different from most others who recorded stories during this period. The Grimms wanted the stories told as they had been for years by mostly uneducated people.

Hans Christian Andersen (1805–1875)

Hans Christian Andersen was born in 1805 in Denmark. While he wrote many plays, novels, and poems, he is most widely known for his fairy tales. Stories such as *The Emperor's New Clothes, The Ugly Duckling, The Princess and the Pea,* and *The Little Mermaid* are deeply embedded in the West's collective consciousness and have inspired ballets, animated films, live–action films, and plays.

His first attempts at writing fairy tales were revisions of stories that he heard as a child, but soon he broke new ground with his style and use of idiom, irony and humor, memorable characters and gentle moral teaching. Andersen's over 200 fairy tales, which have been translated into more than 125 languages, are greatly beloved by children while the abiding lessons of virtue and resilience in the face of adversity resonate for mature readers as well. Though they do not all end happily, his *Fairy Tales* resound with an authenticity that only unabashed sincerity can produce from a man who could still see through a child's eyes.

H. C. Andersen's fairy tales also contain autobiographical details of the man himself. He was the only son of washerwoman and a shoemaker. Young Hans grew to be tall and lanky, awkward and effeminate, but he loved to sing and dance, and he had a vivid imagination.

Mark Twain (1835–1910)

Samuel Clemens (aka Mark Twain) was an American author and raconteur who was famous not only for his popular books like *Huckleberry Finn, Tom Sawyer,* and *The Prince and the Pauper,* but also for his live presentations. In many ways he was the perfect model for the modern–day storyteller. He wrote great, original stories, imbued with biting wit and charm and also an underlying message, which was basically don't be an ass. He would travel around the U.S. and many parts of the world giving these extremely popular one–night only shows where he, alone on stage with just a table, a cigar and a glass of water, was the entire show. He held audiences spellbound with his stories and anecdotes that featured his unique and humorous perspective on issues of his time. In the 1970's the American actor Hal Holbrook donned stage make–up, a grey wig and a white suit and created an extremely popular one–man show called "Mark Twain Tonight" that was basically a recreation of Twain's traveling show.

Mark Twain is often quoted because of his wonderful humor and for the pithiness of the wisdom within. They are great to sprinkle into your stories because they can make you look to be as funny and wise as he was. As Mark Twain once said, "If you tell the truth, you don't have to remember anything."

(See what I mean?)

Edgar Allan Poe (1809-1849)

Edgar Allan Poe, like Hans Christian Andersen and a few others on our list, may not have actually "told" stories per se, as much as he wrote them. This book, of course, is attempting to illustrate that a good portion of being a good storyteller is to have a good story to tell. We need to both WRITE a good story and to TELL it well.

Say the name Edgar Allan Poe and people think of scary stories like *The Pit and the Pendulum, The Tell-Tale Heart,* and *The Cask of Amontillado.* Poe's name is synonymous with horror and yet he virtually invented the genre of detective stories when he published *The Murders in the Rue Morgue* in 1841. He was also a great poet. His poem, *The Raven,* is considered a great American literary work and made him a literary sensation when published in 1845. In the work, Poe explored some of his common themes—death and loss.

Curiously, the circumstances of his own death are also cloaked in mystery. In September of 1849, Poe left Richmond, Virginia, on his way home to New York. He didn't make it.

About a week later, he stumbled into a tavern in Baltimore too delirious to tell anyone what had happened to him. He looked terrible. He was incoherent and wearing dirty clothes that were not his own. He was taken to the hospital and died a few days later. Theories as to what caused Poe's death include suicide, murder, influenza, and that Poe was a victim of "cooping"—a form of 19th century voter fraud where people were kidnapped and forced to vote several times against their will, often in disguise—a description that matches Poe's that day.

He wrote wicked good stories

Storytellers in the 20th Century

 Those who tell the stories rule the world.

—Hopi Native American proverb

Previous: Ancient Storyteller, by Amrita Sher-Gil, 1940

Milton H. Erickson, M.D. (1901– 1980)

Milton Erickson, M.D. was not only the greatest hypnotherapist of the 20th century, he was also one of the most influential psychotherapists of that time. His innovative, solution–focused therapy departed markedly from the traditional Freudian–inspired methodologies of his day and influenced scores of more modern approaches like Solution-Focused Brief therapy, Neuro-Linguistic Programming, and—of course—Ericksonian Hypnosis and Psychotherapy.

One of the main unique characteristics of his approach was his use of storytelling. In Ericksonian Hypnotherapy, these stories are referred to as Therapeutic Metaphors and are told to impart a lesson or learning that is designed to be relevant and important for the listener. In this way one might say, "Ah...that's just like Aesop's fables." And in a way you'd be right. However, Erickson's teaching tales were generally more subtle than Aesop's stories and the lesson or "moral of the story" was left up to the listener to figure out for him or herself. Erickson's famous refrain to "Trust your Unconscious mind" allowed for multiple interpretations of the same story when heard by different people, yet each interpretation was right for each listener from their perspective

Another difference from Aesop's fables is that Erickson's stories were rarely about imaginary animals that could talk. Erickson tended to utilize anecdotal stories from his own life experience or experiences with previous patients.

In addition to the meaning of the story, Erickson was also keenly aware of the power of words and HOW those words were spoken. Because he was doing hypnotherapy in an indirect way, the hypnotic suggestions would often be subtly woven into the story so that the listener might not ever realize—consciously—that these suggestions were being given.

Walt Disney (1901–1966)

"I would rather entertain and hope that people learned something than educate people and hope they were entertained."

Walt Disney created Mickey Mouse in 1928, produced the world's first animated feature film, *Snow White and the Seven Dwarfs*, in 1937, opened Disneyland in 1955, and along the way became one of the most iconic figures of the 20th century.

"My entertainment credo has not changed a whit. Strong combat and soft satire are in our story cores. Virtue triumphs over wickedness in our fables. Tyrannical bullies are routed or conquered by our good little people, human or animal. Basic morality is always deeply implicit in our screen legends. But they are never sappy or namby–pamby. And they never prate or preach. All are pitched toward the happy and satisfactory ending. There is no cynicism in me and there is none allowed in our work."

Walt Disney and his brother Roy formed "Disney Brothers Studios" in 1923 and soon changed the name to "Walt Disney Studios." Mickey Mouse made his official debut in a 1928 short film titled "Steamboat Willie," one of the first cartoons ever to use synchronized sound effects. Walt, himself, supplied Mickey's voice. On December 21, 1937, Walt Disney Studios released *Snow White and the Seven Dwarfs*, the first full–length animated musical feature. Over the next five years, they completed other full–length animated classics including *Pinocchio, Fantasia, Dumbo,* and *Bambi.*

Ever the innovator, Walt Disney's dream of the first–ever theme park came true when Disneyland Park opened in 1955. Walt also became a television pioneer, beginning television production in 1954, and was among the first to present full–color programming with his *Wonderful World of Color* in 1961.

By the way, rumors about him being cryogenically frozen after death are false. His remains were cremated and interred at Forest Lawn Memorial Park in Glendale, California. It is, however, a good story.

Ernest Hemingway (1899–1961)

Legend has it that one day in the 1920s, Ernest Hemingway was in a nightclub in Cuba having a rollicking night out drinking with his literary friends. The subject of writing inevitably came up and challenges were made to Hemingway's famous lean, terse sentences. The discussion culminated when one of his colleagues bet him that he couldn't write a complete story in just six words. They paid up. Hemingway is said to have considered it his best work. This is what he wrote:

"For Sale: Baby shoes — never worn."

This story, factual or fanciful, has inspired many other people to come up with their own six word stories, even crystalizing their whole lives into six-word memoirs.

Great Movie Makers

It is an easy argument to make that film, television and other forms of video have become the predominant storytelling medium in recent years. And yet it is the quality of the story being told in those visual media that set good ones apart from the boatloads of forgettable dreck that are offered up.

Great storytellers who have made memorable movies include the following. I'm sure this following list is non–exhaustive and you undoubtedly have your own list that may well be better than ours.

Ingmar Bergman
A Swedish director, writer and producer who worked in film, television, and theatre. He is recognized as one of the most accomplished and influential auteurs of all time and is most famous for films such as *The Seventh Seal, Wild Strawberries, Persona, Cries and Whispers*, and *Fanny and Alexander*.

Frank Capra
Sentimental but not sappy, his best movies (*Mr. Smith Goes to Washington, It's a Wonderful Life*) wrap dark themes in happy endings.

Charlie Chaplin
He was a genius of silent comedy and one of its first stars. *The Tramp* and *Modern Times* are still comic icons.

Claire Denis
France's greatest living female film director. Following her acclaimed debut, *Chocolat*, she's continued to explore French colonial themes in her multi–award–winning films such as *Beau Travail, White Material,* and *35 Shots of Rum.*

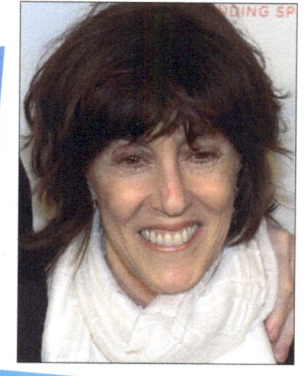

Nora Ephron
An renowned essayist and novelist who wrote screenplays for several popular films, all featuring strong female characters. Among them: *Silkwood, Heartburn, When Harry Met Sally, Sleepless in Seattle, You've got Mail.*

Federico Fellini
An Italian film director and screenwriter. Known for his distinct style that blends fantasy and baroque images with earthiness, he is recognized as one of the most influential filmmakers of all time.

Alfred Hitchcock
A master of suspense and gallows humor, he turned out classic after classic, including *Vertigo, Psycho,* and *The Birds.*

Bottom Line: The quality of the movie is only as good as the quality of the story. Obviously, good screenplays can get poor treatments and not become a good movie, and less–than–great screenplays can be made into movies with huge budgets and sell lots of tickets, but I will wager that without a good story, the popularity of those movies won't last.

Speaking of Stories and Movies: Robert McKee

One man, perhaps more than anyone else, has done more for getting this message across to movie makers since the early 1980s when he began offering his now famous STORY Seminar class. Robert McKee (born 1941) is a creative writing instructor who is widely known for his popular "Story Seminar," which he developed when he was a professor at the University of Southern California. McKee is the author of a "screenwriters' bible" called *Story: Substance, Structure, Style and the Principles of Screenwriting.* Online, McKee has a blog and a writers' resource website called "Storylogue."

McKee's "Story Seminar" runs twice yearly in New York, Los Angeles, and London, and about once yearly in other major cities worldwide including Amsterdam, Beijing, Mumbai, Paris, and Rio de Janeiro. The seminar covers how story fits the human mind, from the philosophical to the structural. McKee's one–day "Genre Seminars," often held 5 days in a row, delve into the conventions of the Thriller, the Comedy, the Love Story, the Action Story, and Television.

Rather than simply handling "mechanical" aspects of fiction technique such as plot or dialogue taken individually, McKee examines the narrative structure of a work and what makes a story compelling or not. This could work equally as well as an analysis of any other genre or form of narrative, whether in screenplay or any other form, and could also encompass nonfiction works as long as they attempt to "tell a story."

American Country Music

American country music is famous for its storytelling. So where did that all come from? Well, country music has a history all its own and has had thousands of artists who told stories in song. Picking any one practitioner of the art as emblematic of the whole is practically an unwinnable proposition. Nevertheless – "fools plunge in where angels fear to tread," so here we go:

Jimmie Rodgers

Jimmie Rodgers was the first person inducted into the Country Music Hall of Fame (1961), and today he is known as the "Father of Country Music." Born in Mississippi in 1897, he was a country singer who became famous for his style of yodeling. Throughout his career, he performed several hit singles, including "Sleep, Baby, Sleep" and "Blue Yodel (T is for Texas)." He later recorded with the legendary jazz musician Louis Armstrong. He was one of the first country superstars.

Although he died young at the age of 35 and his recording career spanned only six years, Rodgers nevertheless had a profound impact on the development of both country music and rock and roll. Bestowed with such nicknames as the Blue Yodeler, the Singing Brakeman and the Father of Country Music, Rodgers' 110 songs about hard work, hard drinking and heartbreak set an emotional tone for country music that has remained its focus to this date. His heavy reliance on African–American blues and jazz set a precedent that shaped the development of both country music and rock and roll over the ensuing decades.

Summing up Rodgers' influence on modern music, folk legend Bob Dylan said, "Jimmie Rodgers, of course, is one of the guiding lights of the 20th century, whose way with song has always been an inspiration to those of us who have followed the path. He was a performer of force without precedent with a sound as lonesome and mystical as it was dynamic. He gives hope to the vanquished and humility to the mighty."

More Great Country Music Songwriters

Country music seeks to transmit authentic human experience. Whether we're in love, in pain, drunk, sober, incarcerated, free…the words of country songwriters attempt to capture the emotions flowing from these states and relate them universally.

1. Hank Williams, Sr.

Another claimant to the title of the Father of Country music, his humble beginnings made him an expert in all subjects: love in *Hey Good Lookin'*, solitude in *I'm So Lonesome I Could Cry* and terror in *I'll Never Get Out of This World Alive*. With Hank, if you're not laughin', you're cryin'.

2. Merle Haggard

Hank may be the father, but Merle is the son. The honesty of songs like *Mama Tried* and *Sing Me Back Home* reverberates throughout us all. Merle's authenticity—from the pain and joy in his heart—changes lives, cementing his claim to country music immortality.

3. Johnny Cash

People who hate country music love Johnny Cash. Country is about talking plain and true to the everyday person. We can all relate to *Folsom Prison Blues* if we've ever been stuck anywhere; that's why it's impossible to keep your foot from tappin' when Johnny comes on.

4. Kris Kristofferson

Who thinks Janis Joplin wrote *Me & Bobby McGee* or that Johnny Cash wrote *Sunday Morning Coming Down?* Everyone can sing along to Kris' songs, whether you know of him or not—and for him, feelin' good is good enough.

5. Willie Nelson

Starting as a clean-cut kid professing traditional values in *Family Bible*, Willie emerged later as an outlaw with new traditions in *Whiskey River*. He changed the way we hear country, showing us it's gritty side alongside all of its sweet serenading.

6. Townes Van Zandt

Townes understands humanity with a simplicity the rest of us never quite grasp. He gives us timeless epics, like *Pancho and Lefty* and optimistic poetry, like *To Live is to Fly*. Townes never conformed to Nashville, and it is his unconventionality that defines his genius.

7. Dolly Parton

After hearing *Coat of Many Colors*, how can you dispute Dolly's genius? Having written over 3,000 songs (seriously!?), she famously denied Elvis the right to cover *I Will Always Love You*–now there's something for the King.

8. Waylon Jennings

Country's all–time rebel, Waylon showed America that country music doesn't need to be sweet. With number–one hits about the darker side of life, like *I Ain't Living Long Like This*, Waylon confirms that heartbreak isn't the only heartache.

9. Guy Clark

They don't call him "The Craftsman" for nothing. Precise songwriting, like *The Cape* and *L.A. Freeway*, combine the rough edges of outlaw country with the tenderness of country's roots, creating a new brand of country music.

10. Steve Earle

Though Steve is a bonafide folkie, he translates life's joys and pains into song with grace. From classics like *Guitar Town* to ballads like *Goodbye*, Steve's unique picking and gut–wrenching lyrics inspire us all to feel more.

Folk Music

Even older and more broadly defined than American county music is "folk" music. In its broadest definition, folk music is the music that anybody who wasn't nobility played, usually on string instruments like guitar, violin or some other, easily carried instrument. Very often the songs sung by folk singers were, like the Grimm Brother's stories, passed down over the years in an oral (and aural) tradition from one musician to the next.

Bob Dylan was one of the first musicians in the folk music revival of the 1950s and 1960s to start writing his own songs that were stylistically in keeping with the folk traditions. He was influenced heavily by the poetic example of Woody Guthrie who traveled the U.S., often by jumping a freight train as many "hobos" did during the Great Depression, singing and collecting songs along the way. Woody Guthrie most famously wrote "This Land is Your Land," a song that became a folk anthem in the 1960s.

Dylan adopted the attitude and aura of Guthrie but mostly wrote his own songs that themselves became iconic masterworks. Songs like "Blowing in the Wind," "All Along the Watchtower," and "Don't Think Twice, It's All Right" are classics from his huge trove of work. Work that, in 2016, earned Dylan the Nobel Prize for Literature.

Radio Storytellers of the 20th Century

Before television seized the mantle, radio was king of the airwaves. It was the mesmerizing medium of the early part of the 20th century. People would sit transfixed around their radios, listening to their favorite shows as a family, or as a group of co-workers. Very much like village storytellers of old, the radio became the source of entertainment, imagination and—also—news from around the world. Certain speeches delivered by political leaders–like Franklin Roosevelt's announcement of the bombing of Pearl Harbor ("...a date that will in infamy") live on today as auditory icons of an era. Here are just some of you might have heard, gathered around the radio with your family back in the 1930s (give or take a decade).

- The Mercury Theatre on the Air/ The War of the Worlds
- The Abbott and Costello Show/ Who's on First
- The Adventures of Philip Marlowe
- The Baby Snooks Show
- Fibber McGee and Molly/ I Can Get It for You Wholesale
- The Burns and Allen Show
- Suspense/Sorry, Wrong Number
- The Saint/The Corpse Said Ouch
- Arthur Godfrey Time
- Walter Winchell Show
- The Adventures of Superman/ Origin Retold
- Dimension X/The Martian Chronicles
- The Eddie Cantor Show
- The Fred Allen Show
- The Jack Benny Program/Money or Your Life
- Dick Tracy
- The Shadow
- The Adventures of Sam Spade, Detective/The Death Bed Caper
- Inner Sanctum Mysteries/ The Shadow of Death
- The Great Gildersleeve
- I Love Lucy
- Suspense/Backseat Driver

Garrison Keillor (born August 7, 1942)

Gary Edward "Garrison" Keillor is an American author, storyteller, humorist, and radio personality. He is known as host of the Minnesota Public Radio show *A Prairie Home Companion* (called *Garrison Keillor's Radio Show* in some international syndication). Keillor created the fictional Minnesota town Lake Woebegone, the setting of many of his books, including *Lake Woebegone Days* and *Leaving Home: A Collection of Lake Woebegone Stories.* Other creations include Guy Noir, whom Keillor also voices, a detective who appears in *A Prairie Home Companion.*

The centerpiece of the show has always been a story told to the audience by Mr. Keillor. There were no sound effects, no music, just Mr. Keillor standing center stage without a script and a microphone on a mic stand. (Even though this was a radio show it was performed in front of a live audience.) He delivered it as news from Lake Wobegone, his home town, and always began the same way;

"It's been a quiet week in Lake Wobegone..." His stories were always quite funny, often moving and always engaging. So much so that this quirky show, broadcast on NPR, lasted for over 40 years.

"We intended the show to last for a year, or maybe two, but just as we were about to quit, the show started to draw an audience, fifty, a hundred, two hundred people coming to see it on Saturday night, and we kept going so we could figure out what we were doing right. The formula is simple: a variety of music that appeals, radio actors who can do noir, or horror, or soap, strong writing, a Midwestern ethos, and the thrill of live radio. And a support staff to do the work. It isn't what I planned to be doing for forty years but luckily for me my plans went awry. It's a good show. People have grown up listening to it and now they are middle-aged and still like it."
— *Garrison Keillor*

Poets, Slam Poets, and Hip Hop Artists

Poets and storytellers have much in common. Obviously, both art forms deal with language. Often, stories or poems are spoken out loud, so the use of the voice, rhythm, and tempo are brought into play. Poems may pay more attention to the words themselves, while stories keep an eye more on the arc of the storyline, but that difference is more of emphasis, rather than black or white contrast. In other words, story arc is as important to a poem as word choice is important to a story.

In our list of great poets of the 20th century up to today, we include *poets* whose work was mostly written and read quietly by individual readers, *slam poets* whose work is mostly performed out loud in front of a live audience, and *hip hop artists* whose work was set to music and both performed live and recorded on disc (or other media). And while our categories are somewhat forced, each of the individuals mentioned below deserve recognition because of their powerful imagery, imaginative use of the English language—sometimes rhyming, sometimes not—and the impact they have had on their art form.

And yet, it is clear to us that attempting to make any sort of "best-of" list is a fool's errand. Many artists who also deserve to be on this list are absent from it, and probably we've included one or two that you believe should not be here. And yet even if we made a list of people we neglected to include in our list, we could probably make an equally large list of other names we left off of THAT list. And if you believe we are just plain wrong to have included some folks whom we have included and total idiots for not including that person you know to be the best of his or her generation we can only say, you're right. Undoubtedly. It's so obvious now that you say so. How could we have missed that? Thank you. Please forgive us. You know what? It's our editor's fault. We agree with YOU.

Poets

Maya Angelou (1928-2014)

Maya Angelou, born Marguerite Annie Johnson, was a Pulitzer Prize–winning African–American poet, but that was just one of her many talents. She was a dancer, singer, actor, civil rights activist, teacher, and author. One of Angelou's most famous works is the poem *On the Pulse of Morning,* which she wrote especially for and recited at President Bill Clinton's inaugural ceremony in January 1993–marking the first inaugural recitation since 1961, when Robert Frost delivered his poem *The Gift Outright* at President John F. Kennedy's inauguration. Angelou went on to win a Grammy Award (best spoken word album) for the audio version of the poem.

Pablo Neruda (1904-1973)

No poet has more passionately and thoroughly spoken for his people than Neruda. *Canto General,* for example, is a 15–part book, comprised of over 200 poems and 15,000 lines. It tries to map the entire history of Latin America. It is an insanely ambitious project that seemed to unify a country. His poems articulated hopes, dreams, desires, histories, protest, sexuality, beauty, and national pride like no one before or since. Because of his poetry he became an ambassador, a statesman, and even his party's candidate for president of Chile. Think about that: a poet so popular, so beloved, a poet with so much cultural cache that he could be a viable candidate for president. And in 1970 no less. Neruda won the Nobel Prize for Literature in 1971.

Alice Walker (Born: February 9, 1944)

Alice Walker is an American poet, activist, author and feminist. Her most famous work, the novel *The Color Purple,* won the National Book Award and the Pulitzer Prize for Fiction and it remains one of the bestselling books in the United States. It has also been made into a popular movie and Broadway play.

Slam Poetry

There's something about hearing a poem being performed that feels like listening to music: the delivery, pitch, and rhythm are tailored to create just the right reaction and hit you in a very specific way. Whether they're talking about their first love, worst job, or unbelievable college experience, these slam poets use language and voice like no one else you've ever heard.

Marc Kelly Smith

M.K. Smith (1949–present) invented the Poetry Slam. Smith started at an open night night at the Get Me High lounge in November 1984 called the Monday Night Poetry Reading. Even as poets scoffed at artists "performing" their work, rather than genteely "reading" it, the event grew in popularity. Smith saw his approach as an "up yours" to establishment poets he considered snooty and effete, because at their events, "no one was listening."

According to Smith, who once attended a conventional reading with his manuscripts concealed inside a newspaper, "The very word 'poetry' repels people. Why is that? Because of what schools have done to it. The slam gives it back to the people... We need people to talk poetry to each other. That's how we communicate our values, our hearts, the things that we've learned that make us who we are."

Taylor Mali

Taylor Mali is one of the best slam poets working today, and has appeared multiple times on teams at the National Poetry Slam. He's probably best known for "What Teachers Make," a poem he wrote a few years ago that's enjoyed a viral popularity ever since.

Alix Olson

Alix Olson's spoken–word performances attack homo-phobia, sexism, and corruption with wit and style. She won the National Poetry Slam Championship in 1998 and has since published her work multiple times and appeared on "Def Poetry Jam" and national tours. She was also the subject of a documentary called *Left Lane: On the Road With Folk Poet Alix Olson*. *America's on Sale* is a great example of her style and subject matter.

Hip Hop

Like we said, there's something about hearing a poem being performed that feels like listening to music. And, in the case of hip hop, you ARE listening to music. It's an amazing blend of poetry and music that is arguably the most vital thing to happen to poetry since, well, ever.

Tupac Shakur

Tupac Shakur, born in New York City, New York on June 16, 1971, was an American rapper. Shakur sold over 75 million albums worldwide, making him one of the best–selling music artists in the world. *Rolling Stone* magazine named him the 86th Greatest Artist of All Time.

Notorious B.I.G.

Christopher George Latore Wallace (May 21, 1972–March 9, 1997), better known by his stage names The Notorious B.I.G, Biggie, or Biggie Smalls, was an American rapper. He is consistently ranked as one of the greatest and most influential rappers of all time. Wallace was raised in the borough of Brooklyn. When he released his debut album *Ready to Die* in 1994, he became a central figure in the East Coast hip hop scene and increased New York's visibility in the genre at a time when West Coast hip hop was dominant in the mainstream. The following year, Wallace led his childhood friends to chart success through his protégé group, Junior M.A.F.I.A. While recording his second album, Wallace was heavily involved in the growing East Coast–West Coast hip hop feud.

Jay-Z

Shawn Corey Carter (born December 4, 1969), known by his stage name Jay Z (formerly Jay–Z), is an American rapper, entrepreneur and investor. He is one of the most financially successful hip hop artists in America. In 2014, Forbes estimated Jay Z's net worth at nearly $520 million. He is one of the world's best–selling artists of all time, having sold more than 100 million records, while receiving 21 Grammy Awards for his musical work and numerous additional nominations. Consistently ranked as one of the greatest rappers ever, he was ranked number one by MTV in their list of The Greatest MCs of All–Time in 2006. Three of his albums, *Reasonable Doubt* (1996), *The Blueprint* (2001), and *The Black Album* (2003), are considered landmarks in the genre with all of them featured in *Rolling Stone's* list of the 500 greatest albums of all time.

Eminem

Marshall Bruce Mathers III (born October 17, 1972), known professionally as Eminem, is an American rapper, songwriter, record producer, and actor from Detroit, Michigan. In addition to his solo career, he is a member of D12, and with Royce da 5'9", is one half of the hip hop duo Bad Meets Evil. Eminem is the best–selling artist of the 2000s in the United States. *Rolling Stone* ranked him 83rd on its list of 100 Greatest Artists of All Time, calling him the King of Hip Hop. Including his work with D12 and Bad Meets Evil, Eminem has had ten number–one albums on the *Billboard* 200. He has sold more than 172 million albums, making him one of the world's best–selling artists. As of June 2014, Eminem is the second–bestselling male artist of the Nielsen SoundScan era, the sixth–bestselling artist in the United States and the bestselling hip hop artist, with sales of 45.1 million albums and 42 million tracks (including 31 million digital single certifications).

One-Person Shows

One-man or one-woman shows could be called "long-form" storytelling because the story being told becomes a whole evening of entertainment. Often the performer will weave a number of anecdotes together within the overarching theme of the show and sometimes adopt widely different personas while acting out the characters to more fully bring the story to life.

There is a distinction between auto-biographical storytelling and allegorical or illustrative storytelling. Some storytellers find material in their personal experiences and the audience places a high value on the truth of the stories being told. Listeners can feel a strong connection to the performer as he or she reveals the soft underbelly of their being to the audience. Others find their material in their imaginations and create characters to illustrate the point they are attempting to make or the experience they are trying to create for the audience.

As an example, contrast these two exemplars of their craft: Spalding Gray and Lily Tomlin. Spalding Gray performed his first monologue in 1977, and in 1985 made his biggest splash with the monologue "Swimming to Cambodia," based primarily on his experiences filming a small role in the 1984 film *The Killing Fields.* Lily Tomlin took her family of personas, both male and female, to Broadway on two occasions: *Lily Tomlin: Appearing Nitely* in 1977 and the Tony-winning *The Search for Signs of Intelligent Life in the Universe* in 1985. Along with her collaborator and life partner Jane Wagner, Tomlin wrote monologues where her characters riffed on life, society and the human condition.

Autobiographical storytelling like Spalding Gray's is often referred to as monologuing (or monologging) and is very different than solo performance like Lily Tomlin's, where the performer steps into a series of characters with different voices and physical characteristics.

Monologuists

Spalding Gray

Spalding Gray started a whole modern-day genre of storytelling as he tapped into his own personal experiences and feelings and seemed to largely extemporize as a stream of consciousness. His stories were often about simple things like fatherhood, marriage, and family ski trips. However, in his most famous work, "Swimming to Cambodia," he told the story of his experiences in Thailand as an actor in a minor role while filming *The Killing Fields.* The story included graphic depictions of how he spent his many free hours during the filming—like an infamous "banana show" in a local nightclub—and accounts he'd heard about or researched about the genocide that was practiced by the fanatical Khmer Rouge on their Cambodian countrymen. He recounts in great and gory detail all of his findings of the disappearance of millions of Cambodians in the greatest mass murder of modern history. This one-man show was made into a movie in 1987 directed by Roland Joffé.

He described his process as being a "collage artist." He would fill grade school composition notebooks with descriptions of his life experiences, thoughts, and reactions. He would then start reviewing it all to see what structure might present itself. Then he booked a date to perform it and as he got closer to that date the more his mind formulated how he would want it to go. But he'd speak it for the first time publicly at that performance.

After that performance, or maybe several performances, he got clear on what the story was and he wrote it down and practiced it. His storytelling style made his stories sound fresh, yet he practiced his delivery so much the performances were virtually the same from night to night. Gray was not afraid to be dramatic. His voice raced through a litany of images, his arms would wave, his eyes would flash. Then sometimes he'd be quiet and contemplative, equally unafraid of silence. He died in 2004, which is a story unto itself.

One of the direct descendants of Mr. Gray's storytelling style is Mike Daisey, who was once described by *The New York Times* as "one of the finest solo performers of his generation." But then he made a major blunder. One of his big stories about the manufacturing of Apple's products in China turned out to be false. A widely listened–to podcast of "This American Life" laid this out plainly and his career took a serious hit. *Don't be like Mike.* Stories don't have to be true to be great entertainment, but if you are *telling* people your story is true, it should be. Instead, be like *this* Mike:

Mike Birbiglia

Mike Birbiglia is a standup comic and storyteller whose one-man shows have played to sold–out theaters on Broadway and around the world. His stories are true and yet, like many a great standup, told through the lens of his unique and hilarious viewpoint. His shows are great examples of how you can take a story and shape it in such a way that it is interesting from moment to moment and also has an overarching structure that keeps the audience engaged until the closing curtain.

Solo Performance

Lily Tomlin

Lily Tomlin made her first big splash when she joined the cast of Rowan & Martin's *Laugh-In* in its third season, introducing audiences to a telephone company employee named Ernestine and a little girl named Edith Ann. After her successful run on *Laugh-In,* Tomlin went on to star in six television comedy specials that she co-wrote with her partner Jane Wagner. Tomlin began her film career a few years later as part of the ensemble of Robert Altman's *Nashville.*

While appearing on the big screen, Tomlin made her Broadway debut in her one-woman show, *Appearing Nitely,* which was written and directed by Wagner. The show incorporated favorite Tomlin roles including Ernestine and housewife Judith Beasley, and introduced new characters such as Trudy the bag lady, Rick the singles bar cruiser and Sister Boogie Woman, a 77-year-old blues revivalist.

Tomlin returned to Broadway in 1985 and won a Tony Award for her performance in her one-woman show *The Search for Signs of Intelligent Life in the Universe,* which was also written by Wagner. After a year-long run on Broadway, the show toured the country, was made into a 1991 film, and revived on Broadway in 2000.

Tomlin continues to perform on screen and TV and continues to gain recognition for her work, being nominated for and receiving numerous awards, including four primetime Emmys for her television work and two Tonys for her one-woman shows. In December 2014 she was one of five honorees for the Kennedy Center Honors.

Anna Deavere Smith

In addition to her work in television and film, Anna Deavere Smith is said to have created a new form of theatre. She typically interviews a wide scope of interesting and unique individuals, usually on a topic of civic and political interest, and then creates theater works in which she performs portions of those interviews as a series of monologues— as many as 52 characters in one production— representing multiple points of view. When granted the prestigious MacArthur Award, her work was described as "a blend of theatrical art, social commentary, journalism, and intimate reverie." Her work has been celebrated simultaneously for its journalistic detail as well as its empathic treatment of the people she portrays. David Richard wrote in *The New York Times* that Anna Deavere Smith "is the ultimate impressionist. She does people's souls."

Whoopi Goldberg

Whoopi Goldberg said that when she tried to start a career in acting there weren't many roles for young women of color, so she wrote one of her own. *The Spook Show,* her one–woman show, was seen by director Mike Nichols who offered to take it to Broadway. Retitled *Whoopi Goldberg* for its Broadway incarnation, the play showcased Goldberg's talent for imitating everyone from valley girls to down–and–out bums. Her stark yet funny monologues recalled Lily Tomlin, but with a streetwise edge, a lot of four–letter words, and uncompromising pathos.

While on Broadway, Goldberg's performance caught the eye of director Steven Spielberg who offered her a leading role in his new movie, *The Color Purple,* which did very well. It was later nominated for 11 Academy Awards, including a nomination for Goldberg as Best Actress. Whoopi Goldberg's multi–faceted career continues and includes a long–running position as host to TV's daytime talk show, *The View.*

Sarah Jones

"Chameleon–like" barely describes the astonishing ease with which Sarah Jones slips in and out of the characters in her solo performances—as many as fourteen personae in her Broadway hit *Bridge & Tunnel.* Critics marvel not only at her ability to perfectly mimic accents and mannerisms, but also to seemingly reshape her body, down to pupils and dimples, in the blink of an eye.

Stand-Up Comics

Stand–up comics are storytellers, but storytellers are not necessarily stand–up comics.

Stand–up is a decidedly American invention, with its roots going back into the mid–1800s. Up until that time comedy was the exclusive domain of theater. The unintentional grandfather of stand–up comedy was Thomas Dartmouth "Daddy" Rice, the man who is credited with inventing the minstrel shows.

Minstrel Shows begat Vaudeville which begat Burlesque which split into smaller venues that featured specialized entertainment. They became music clubs, off–off Broadway theaters, and even strip clubs. Comics would often come out between the acts and have to just stand up in front of the curtain. Comics, who used to be jugglers, or singers, or dancers, in addition to being funny, now had a specialty all their own.

The first generation of "stand–ups" included Lenny Bruce, Lord Buckley, Dick Gregory, Bob Newhart, Bill Cosby, and Mort Sahl. These stand–ups, and many others, evolved the craft, and passed it down to Richard Pryor, Freddie Prinze, Joan Rivers and George Carlin. Since the 1970s, stand–up comedy has grown into a huge art form with superb performers and styles too numerous to mention.

In the section of this book entitled "Tell your story like a Stand–Up Comic," we look at how storytellers can learn a lot from joke tellers. A joke's setup, timing and punchline all have their corresponding structural elements in a good story, even if that story is not intended to be funny. It is also true that when a good stand–up comic tells a joke, the response of the audience is a direct result on the comic's ability to tell it well, not just the quality of the joke itself.

George Denis Patrick Carlin
(May 12, 1937–June 22, 2008) was an American stand–up comedian, actor, social critic and author. Carlin was noted for his black comedy and his thoughts on politics, the English language, psychology, religion, and various taboo subjects. Carlin and his "Seven dirty words" comedy routine were central to the 1978 U.S. Supreme Court case *F.C.C. v. Pacifica Foundation*, in which a 5–4 decision affirmed the government's power to regulate indecent material on the public airwaves.

Christopher Julius "Chris" Rock III

is an American comedian, actor, screenwriter, producer, and director. After working as a stand–up comic and appearing in small film roles, Rock came to wider prominence as a cast member of *Saturday Night Live* in the early 1990s. He went on to more prominent film roles, and a series of acclaimed comedy specials for HBO. He was voted the fifth–greatest stand–up comedian in a poll conducted by Comedy Central.

Craig Ferguson

is a Scottish–born American television host, stand–up comedian, writer, actor, director, author, producer and voice artist. He was the host of *The Late Late Show with Craig Ferguson,* an Emmy Award–nominated, Peabody Award–winning late–night talk show that aired on CBS from 2005 to 2014. Ferguson began hosting the syndicated *Celebrity Name Game* in September 2014.

Eddie Izzard

is an English stand–up comedian, actor and writer. Her comedic style takes the form of rambling, whimsical monologue and self–referential pantomime. She had a starring role in the television series *The Riches* as Wayne Malloy and has appeared in many films such as *Ocean's Twelve, Ocean's Thirteen, Mystery Men* and more.

Sarah Silverman

is an American stand–up comedian, writer, producer and actress. Her satirical comedy addresses social taboos and controversial topics, such as racism, sexism and religion, having her comic character endorse them in an ironic fashion. Silverman was a writer and occasional performer for 18 weeks on *Saturday Night Live* and starred in and produced *The Sarah Silverman Program,* which ran from 2007 to 2010 on Comedy Central.

Speech-Givers:
Political, Motivational, Business, and Spiritual

Storytelling is a vital part of being able to capture people's imaginations, spur them to action, and have them continue to feel motivated towards ongoing accomplishment.

This is, of course, the shared objective of preachers, presidents and salesmen. The speech–giver can recite statistics, facts, and figures all day long, but what audiences will remember and be stirred by are the stories that are told that illustrate those facts and figures and bring them to life in their imaginations. The better the speaker is at telling a good story well, the more persuasive they will be and the more success they will enjoy.

Here are just some people who have excelled in this over the years.

Steve Jobs

Steve Jobs, the founder of Apple computer, was famous for his keynote speeches. Whether launching a new product like the iPhone or making an announcement about the direction of the company, he agonized for hours over the details of his presentations. People were amazed at his ability to craft a narrative, to create and maintain suspense, and to deliver a solid message. It wasn't dazzling special effects or crazy props, it was storytelling.

Tony Robbins

Tony Robbins is an American motivational speaker with a difference. Starting as a trainer of NLP with his trademark Firewalk Experience, and evolving into a worldwide phenomenon, Tony Robbins has created an empire of hugely successful seminars, books and audio recordings that is unmatched.

Throughout it all, Tony is a consummate storyteller who unashamedly manipulates his audience's emotional states in an effort to have them experience a breakthrough of their limiting belief systems and create new, empowering associations. Or something like that. Good stuff, for sure.

Franklin D. Roosevelt

One of America's greatest Presidents, FDR was a master of the new media of radio. His "fireside chats" that he broadcast to every living room in America during the 1930s were actually broadcast from a microphone covered desk either from the White House or from Roosevelt's library at his home in Hyde Park. However, the name perfectly evoked the comforting intent behind Roosevelt's words, as well as their informal, conversational tone. Roosevelt took care to use the simplest possible language, concrete examples and analogies in the fireside chats, so as to be clearly understood by the largest number of Americans. He began many of the chats with the greeting "My friends," and referred to himself as "I" and the American people as "you" as if addressing his listeners directly and personally. So, while he didn't tell stories in the same way as many other of our exemplars did, he very successfully painted pictures in people's minds that helped restore the confidence of a nation.

Billy Graham

All religious leaders deliver sermons, although they may use a different word for it, and they all have the same outcome when they tell their stories—to inspire and motivate their followers to adopt or more fully live by their religions' tenets. Christian ministers,

of course, borrow heavily from that most famous of storytellers, Jesus of Nazareth (see the section on early storytellers). Some preachers can get very passionate and colorful in their preaching. The archetypal "Fire and Brimstone" preachers are prime examples of that genre. When *Preaching Magazine* cited the most influential preachers of the 20th century, Billy Graham came in at number two, while a recent LifeWay survey of the most influential preachers ranked Graham at number one.

Barack Obama

The 44th president of the United States, Barack Hussein Obama could easily owe his presidency to his unmatched gift for oratory. His keynote speech at the 2004 Democratic Convention vaulted him into the consciousness of the American public and four years later his 2008 speech on race saved his faltering presidential campaign and catapulted him into the oval office. Obama's best oratory is beautifully

written, meticulously crafted and theatrically delivered. "I don't know of any president who has put that kind of work into his speeches," says Douglas Brinkley, a presidential historian.

Illustration for Annancy Stories, by Pamela Colman Smith, 1899

Storytelling Today

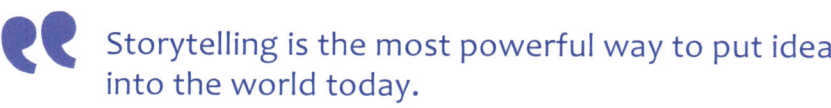 Storytelling is the most powerful way to put ideas into the world today.

—Robert McKee

Storytelling Events and Story Telling People

Picture this: You are sitting on the porch with folks telling stories. It gets dark and the porch light goes on. Soon a moth or two is circling the bulb as the stories continue into the night. That is the origin story of "The Moth," a storytelling phenomenon that attracts thousands of listeners and storytellers to its live events and recorded broadcasts. "RISK!," another storytelling venue, regularly sells out their wildly entertaining shows. Storytelling is everywhere. "World Storytelling Day" is every March 20 – because – why not? It has its roots in a national day for storytelling in Sweden in 1991 and is growing fast. There are many wonderful and popular storytelling events all over the world.

Here are just a few events of note...

The official logo for World Storytelling Day

Storytelling Events

The MOTH

Since its launch in 1997, The Moth has presented thousands of stories told live and without notes in cities all over the English-speaking world. "The Moth Radio Hour" features their most beloved tales and the stories behind the stories. The series debuted in 2009 and is now airing on more than four hundred stations across America. Moth shows are renowned for the great range of human experience they showcase. Each show starts with a theme and the storytellers explore it, often in unexpected ways. Since each story is true and every voice authentic, the shows dance between documentary and theater, creating a unique, intimate, and often enlightening experience for the audience.

Moth Mainstage

Curated events featuring five tellers who develop and shape their stories with thier directors. Beyond theater, The Moth Mainstage is a community where entertainment and enlightenment merge. There is also a competitive element in the Moth world.

StorySLAM

Open-mic storytelling competitions. Open to anyone with a five-minute story to share on the night's theme. Come tell a story, or just enjoy the show!

GrandSLAM

After ten StorySLAMs in a city, the winners then compete for the title of GrandSLAM Champion with a brand new story. This is the ultimate battle of wits and words.

The MOTH presents a few different kinds of shows throughout the year.

RISK!

Similar to the Moth, "RISK!" is a live show and podcast "where people tell true stories they never thought they'd dare to share in public" hosted by Kevin Allison, of the legendary TV sketch comedy troupe *The State.* The award–winning live show happens monthly in New York and Los Angeles. It has featured people like Janeane Garofalo, Lisa Lampanelli, Kevin Nealon, Margaret Cho, Marc Maron, Sarah Silverman, Lili Taylor, Rachel Dratch, Andy Borowitz and more, dropping the act and showing a side of themselves we've never seen before. The weekly podcast gets around a million downloads each month. Slate.com called it "jaw–dropping, hysterically funny, and just plain touching."

The National Storytelling Festival

In contrast to the Moth's emphasis on "true and authentic," more traditional storytelling venues like the National Storytelling Festival in the United States focuses more on the "good and interesting."

Over 40 years ago, a high school journalism teacher and a carload of students heard Grand Ole Opry regular Jerry Clower spin a tale over the radio about coon hunting in Mississippi. And the teacher, Jimmy Neil Smith, had a sudden inspiration: Why not have a storytelling festival right here in northeast Tennessee?

On a warm October weekend in 1973 in historic Jonesborough, the first National Storytelling Festival was held. Hay bales and wagons were the stages, and audience and tellers together didn't number more than 60. It was tiny, but something happened that weekend that forever changed our culture, this traditional art form, and the little Tennessee town.

Produced by the International Storytelling Center, the three–day outdoor festival features performances by internationally known artists and has been hailed as "the leading event of its kind in America." In existence for nearly forty years, the Festival attracts more than 10,000 audience members to Jonesborough—Tennessee's oldest town— from across the United States and the world annually, including school groups whose students attend as an educational experience.

The festival builds on the Appalachian cultural tradition of storytelling. Held under circus tents scattered throughout Jonesborough, storytellers sit on stages or at the head of the tent to perform. There are usually five or six tents in close proximity so that festival goers can easily walk from tent to tent and from performance to performance.

Regaling the audience at the National Storytelling Festival

Story Telling People

We hope it goes without saying that we are leaving out almost everybody who should be included here. We are well aware that there are great storytellers in every county in the world and our infinitesimally small sampling doesn't even *begin* to do justice to the vast number of excellent, wonderful and important storytellers out there.

We are including this section at all because it must be represented. Storytellers are great and great ones are greater still. They must have, at the very least, a section in the book. So that being said, here is a very small sprinkling of notable storytellers...keeping in mind that all the singers and poets and performers and everyone already mentioned in this book could also be included in this section.

Noa Baum

Noa Baum is an award–winning storyteller, born and raised in Jerusalem. Noa combines Jewish folktales, literary adaptations and personal stories that are uplifting and entertaining.

Noa weaves a rich tapestry of wisdom stories from around the world that build understanding between people. One reviewer from Seeds of Peace said, "Noa Baum mesmerized a theater full of some of the harshest critics I know, teenagers from conflict areas of the world. She puts her heart and soul into her work that is rich with meaning and humor."

Noa is the winner of the Parents' Choice Recommended Award, a Storytelling World Award, and recipient of numerous Individual Artist Awards from the Maryland State Arts Council. She's performed at The Kennedy Center, the World Bank, Hebrew University in Jersalem, Bradeis and Stanford Universities and many many other venues.

Daniel Morden

Daniel Morden has delighted audiences all over the world with his performances—from the Arctic to the Pacific to the Caribbean. He has toured widely with The Devil's Violin Company, integrating music with story. His stories are broadcast regularly on BBC radio Wales and BBC Choice TV. He is the author of six books.

Daniel Morden tells traditional tales, stories of the imperfect hero who "stumbles on the path, takes the long way home through the dark forest where the wolves wait, and the shadows whisper. When we finally get home we have a story to tell—a proper tale! It's the twists and turns that make the pattern beautiful."

The BBC has said, "To experience Daniel Morden in full flight is an amazing thing. He combines the troubadour, the actor, the bard, the stand-up comedian and the preacher in the pulpit. One of the UK's greatest storytellers."

Daniel Morden's performances of Greek myth with Hugh Lupton won the Classical Association Award in 2006 for "the most significant contribution to the public understanding of the classics." Morden has twice won the English-language section of the Welsh Books Council's Tir na n-Og Awards, first in 2007 for *Dark Tales from the Woods*, based on Welsh folktales, and then in 2013 for *Tree of Leaf and Flame*, a collection of stories retelling the *Mabinogion*.

Matthew Dicks

As of this writing, Matthew Dicks is a 53-time Moth StorySLAM champion and seven-time Moth GrandSLAM champion. He is an internationally bestselling author of novels like *Memoirs of an Imaginary Friend* and the fantastic and highly recommended book on storytelling, *Storyworthy*. Matthew is a columnist, podcaster, playwright, and an elementary school teacher. He teaches storytelling and public speaking and consults with advertising agencies, filmmakers, and writers. If you ever want to feel lazy, stand next to Matthew.

David Gonzalez

With speech, sound, mime, dance, and above all, inspired imagination, nationally acclaimed master storyteller/performer David Gonzalez is keeping the ancient art of storytelling alive. From London's Royal National Theater to Broadway to hundreds of schools across North America, Gonzalez has performed to more than 5,000 audiences worldwide. A winner of the Helen Hayes Performing Artist of the Year Award, Gonzalez is applauded for his vocal, physical and narrative talents and gift for mimicry, comic timing, and wordplay. Relying on the majesty and variety of language, the limitless landscape of imagination, the pulse of music and the beauty of art, he creates and performs multimedia productions that capture audiences of all ages and cultures.

Jan Blake

Jan Blake is one of the world's leading story-tellers, having performed at storytelling and literature festivals worldwide for over twenty-five years. Born in England of Jamaican heritage, and specializing in stories from Africa, the Caribbean, and Arabia, she has a reputation for dynamic and generous storytelling.

She both teaches and performs storytelling in a wide variety of settings. From children's productions at the Royal Shakespeare Company, through master classes on the educational use of story with the British Council, to storytelling about sustainability for business leaders with the World Wildlife Fund—engaging both children and adults in an unforgettable experience.

Her own storytelling company and school is the Akua Storytelling Project. Jan Blake co-wrote *Give Me My Yam!* (1998), a picture book for young children, and is currently working on several other books.

Ivory storyteller carving from the Qing dynasty (1644-1912)

Part II
WRITING Your Story

Finding Your Story

Inside each of us is a natural-born storyteller, waiting to be released.

—Robin Moore

What IS a Story?

A dictionary might define **story** as an accounting of people and events, real or imaginary. But more than just an accounting of events, a story is told for a *reason*...to illustrate a lesson learned, to develop a sense of community, or to captivate and enthrall the listener's imagination.

What is the secret to making your story captivating?

I'll tell you in a minute...
   wait for it...
      wait for it...

        ...

OK – here it is! The big secret revealed...

    (. . . *drumroll please.* . .)

The big secret of how to make a story work is... to hook the listener's CURIOSITY. Our brains are wired with a desire to find out *what happens next*. When a person finds out what happens next, they feel pleasure as they get a shot of the neurotransmitter *dopamine*–their reward for following through to the end.

Think about it this way:

A STORY is...
how what happens affects someone
who is in pursuit of a challenging goal
and how he or she changes as a result.

When you do that – *and* elicit from your listener the internal question of "What happens next?" – you've got yourself a *story*.

A Ghost Story, by Walter MacEwen, 1891

Serving It Up in all Shapes and Sizes

That being said, what form your story takes is up to you. As we've seen, Hemingway wrote a story in six words. You can have a horror story in two sentences. Your story can be great in five minutes or it could be a full-length epic.

It's like eating a meal. You could just grab something from the fridge and wolf it down on the way to work. That's fine. Sometimes that's all you need. No problem. Or you could enjoy a wondrous meal that delights and draws you into it with its scintillating aromas, it's captivating pairing and contrasting of flavors, all presented in the perfect pacing.

They are both good and do the job of satisfying that human need.

And, just like a chef can take your basic burger and turn it into a gastronomic delight, we, as storytellers, can take a basic, "I did this, then I did this, then this happened," narrative and turn it into something with far more significance and meaning.

Furthermore, like fine dining, a fine story experience will be comprised from both the story itself and from *how it is delivered.*

In this section of the book, we will offer some guidelines for both of these elements of the storyteller's art… how to prepare a great meal and how to serve it with style!

Improving Your Story

The first essential—the life and soul, so to speak, of a story, is the plot.

—Aristotle

Opposite: The Historian, by E. Irving Couse, 1902

Storytelling boils down to two things:

1st Have a good story
2nd Tell it well

In this section of the book you'll learn to do both.

> "There are three rules for writing a novel. Unfortunately, no one knows what they are."
> –Somerset Maugham

Stories come in all shapes and sizes, from the short, amusing anecdote to the epic novel or full–length movie. In all cases what makes for a successful story is the ability to GRAB your audience from the outset and HOLD their attention till the very end.

This requires two things:

1. A good story (aka: a *well-crafted* story)

2. The ability to tell it well

Of course, a great storyteller can take a very mundane story and make it sound fascinating, but how much better would it be if the material were good to start with?

So, we're going to start by looking at the question: how do you craft your story in the first place?

Opposite: A storyteller reciting from the Arabian Nights, 1911

1ST: Craft a Good Story

Let's start at the very beginning.

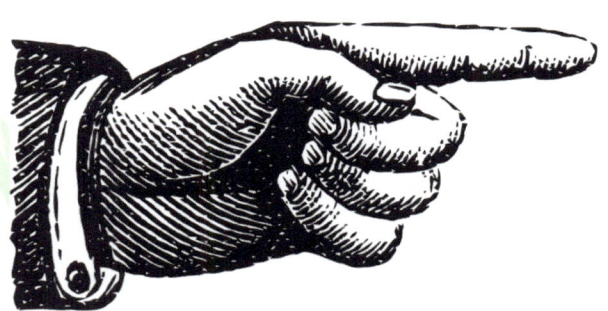

As an example, our friends at The Moth suggest you do NOT start like this: *"So I was thinking about climbing this mountain. But then I watched a little TV and made a snack and took a nap and my mom called and vented about her psoriasis then I did a little laundry (a whites load) (I lost another sock, darn it!) and then I thought about it again and decided I'd climb the mountain the next morning."*

Instead, DO start like this: *"The mountain loomed before me. I had my hunting knife, some trail mix and snow boots. I had to make it to the little cabin and start a fire before sundown or freeze to death for sure."*

Yep. That kind of opening line will do the trick nicely, thank you very much.

1. Create a Strong Opening

Grab their attention and make them *curious*

A. Set the Scene
Where are you? What's happening? Include information like what you see, hear, feel, or smell. Maybe tell us how old you are and who you are with.

B. Establish the *Stakes*
By "stakes" we mean what do you (or the main character in the story) stand to gain or lose? Why is what happens in the story important to you?

C. Have a Great First Line
Sometimes a great first line can both set the scene and establish the stakes at the same time. Succinctness is *golden*.

2. Have Something Happen

3. Resolve the Story

"The Inciting Incident"

Basically, something needs to happen so your story goes somewhere. The change can be subtle or be big and dramatic. It can be positive or negative but it gives the main character a goal he or she can't turn away from.

Like in the classic story form, "Boy finds girl, boy loses girl," the hero of the story finds something that promises great happiness, then an impediment to that happiness pops up and rest of the story is about how the hero must work hard to reclaim that happiness.

The inciting incident should happen early in your story but not necessarily right out of the gate. In a play it is always in the first act, but sometimes right near the end of the first act. In a five minute story told at a Moth, as an example, you should get to it early on. It's how you grab the audience.

FINISH STRONG "Tie it up in a bow"

Avoid meandering endings. It is a good idea to bring your story back to the theme you introduced at the beginning of the story and to resolve the stakes you had set up. After all, the classic story form we mentioned before finishes like this: "Boy finds girl, boy loses girl, *boy wins girl back.*"

Later, when you are actually telling your story, decide exactly what your last line will be and practice that. (NOTE: We're not saying you should start your *writing* process knowing what your last line will be, but when you are done writing get very clear on your last line. Much can be forgiven in the middle of the story if you start strong and end strong.)

HINT:

Throughout your story, edit out some things, embellish others.

As Joyce Carol Oates wrote, "Storytelling is shaped by two contrary, yet complementary, impulses—one toward brevity, compactness, artful omission; the other toward expansion, amplification, enrichment."

A. Don't be a Reporter

Many people mistakenly believe that telling a story means to relate every detail—to give a full accounting of everything that happened exactly as it happened. *Wrong.* This could not be further from the truth.

In fact, in telling a good story you sometimes have to leave out as much as you put in. Maybe even more. As a writer or teller of tales, it's your job to select only the details needed to make your story a good one.

B. *And,* at the same time, spin out certain threads

That's right, embellish! Pick a few decorative threads to spin into a more sparkling web. It's the opposite element to story's tendency to focus or simplify itself. There is also a pure delight in the art of the tale, the tongue of whimsy, the gift of gab in an enchanting, charming way.

Polishing Your Story

 Half my life is an act of revision.
—John Irving

More About Story Structure

A Story's Arc

Listen for structure in stories and you'll find it. It's there. And if it is it a story that resonates over time, you can be certain it has a solid structure to it. Another way to think about structure is the story's "arc."

Here are some ways you can shape a story:

Freytag's Pyramid

Gustav Freytag was a 19th Century German novelist and playwright. He represented dramatic structure in the form of an equilateral triangle, which came to be known as Freytag's Pyramid.

In his model, the plot of a story consists of five parts: exposition, rising action, climax, falling action, and dénouement.

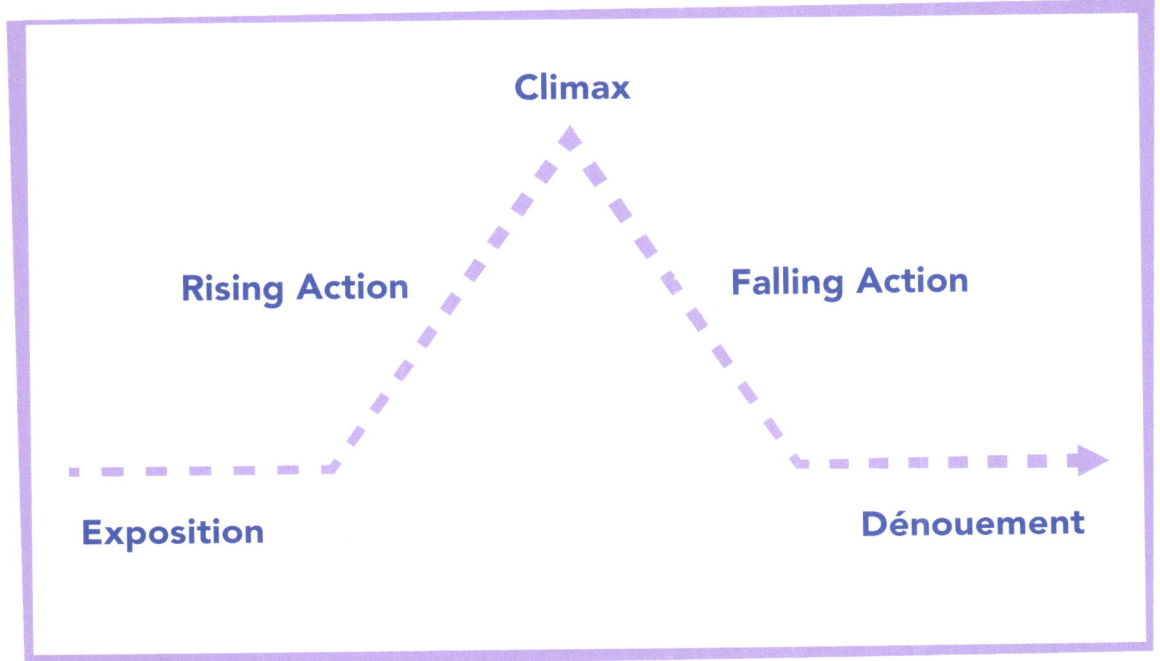

Kurt Vonnegut on Story Arcs

Kurt Vonnegut was an American author best known for the novels *Cat's Cradle*, *Slaughterhouse-Five* and *Breakfast of Champions*. He once gave a very brief lecture where he talked about the importance of story arcs. Vonnegut drew graphs of three classic story arcs with a vertical "G–I axis," which represents the good or ill fortunes of the main character, and a horizontal "B–E" axis that represent the story from beginning to end. The following archetypal story arcs have been used in countless story plots, many of which have translated into movie scripts.

Man in Hole

In this arc somebody gets in trouble, gets out of it again, and ends up better off than where they started. Vonnegut comments, "You see this story again and again. People love it, and it is not copyrighted." You will notice that when this story arc is used in a longer form story, like the movie *Cast Away* with Tom Hanks, there can be a lot of little subplots tucked within the overall arc.

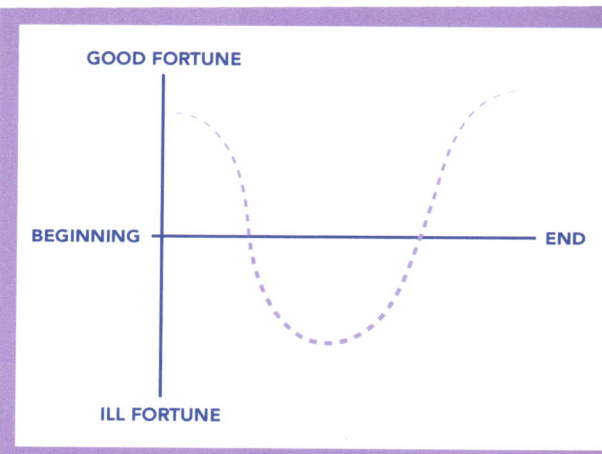

Boy Loses Girl

A close variant to Man in Hole is "Boy Loses Girl," in which a person gets something amazing, loses it, and then gets it back again. Again, this arc has been the blueprint for millions of stories over the years with *Romeo and Juliet* being, perhaps, the most classic example (although that version has a twist at the end that makes it into a bit of a tragedy). Of course, the storyline can just as well be "boy loses boy" or "girl loses girl" or any other such variation. The movie *Slumdog Millionaire* is a great example of a variation of the story plot where the main character is about to win a million dollars on a game show, then has that possibility ripped away from him, and then gets it back. The key to this arc is that there is a sense of loss and reparation which creates the rising and falling dynamics in the storyline.

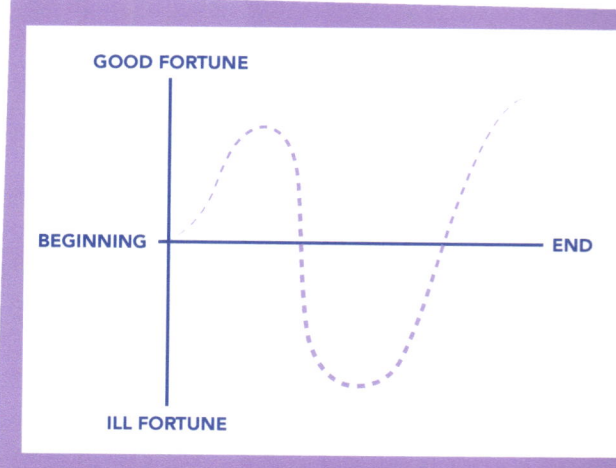

Cinderella

This is one of the most popular stories ever told. The story starts down close to the bottom of the G–I axis with a teenage girl. Her mother has died, so she is understandably feeling sad. Her father remarries an unpleasant new wife with two mean daughters who treat this girl like a servant. A party is arranged at the palace and Cinderella is tasked with getting the mother and sisters prepared, but not permitted to attend herself. As Vonnegut says:

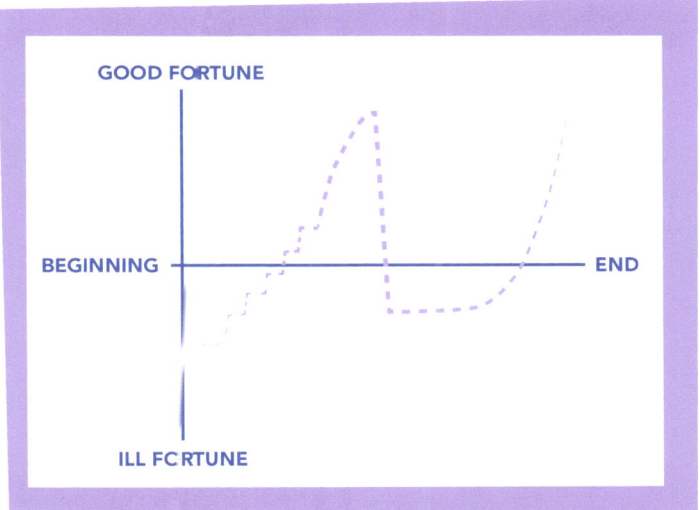

"Her fairy godmother shows up, gives her pantyhose, mascara, and a means of transportation to get to the party. This creates an incremental rise up the G–I axis. Better still, when the girl shows up to this fancy party, she's the belle of the ball, placing her storyline now near the top of that G–I axis. She is so heavily made up that her relatives don't even recognize her. Then the clock strikes twelve, as promised, and it's all taken away again. It doesn't take long for a clock to strike twelve times, so she drops down. Does she drop down to the same level? Absolutely not. No matter what happens after that, she'll remember when the prince was in love with her and she was the belle of the ball. So she meanders along, at her considerably improved level, no matter what, and the shoe fits, and she becomes off-scale happy forevermore."

Joseph Campbell and the Hero's Journey

In mythologist Joseph Campbell's most famous book, *The Hero with a Thousand Faces*, he outlined what he believed to be the basic stages of the mythic cycle, or story arc, of a hero's adventure. Certainly you can find this cycle in many of the epic Greek myths and in J.R.R. Tolkein's *The Lord of the Rings.* This revelation has come to be widely accepted and has been a major influence on many artists, writers and film-makers, including George Lucas' Star Wars movies.

The Hero's Journey

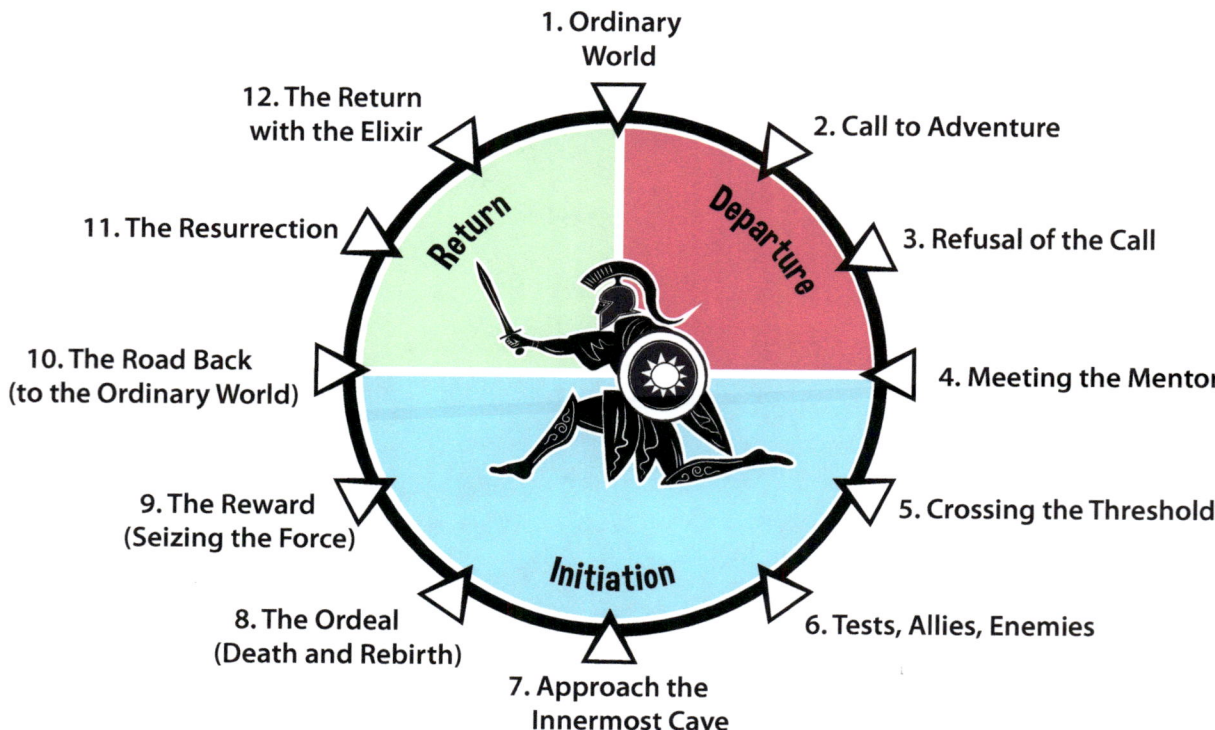

1. Ordinary World
2. Call to Adventure
3. Refusal of the Call
4. Meeting the Mentor
5. Crossing the Threshold
6. Tests, Allies, Enemies
7. Approach the Innermost Cave
8. The Ordeal (Death and Rebirth)
9. The Reward (Seizing the Force)
10. The Road Back (to the Ordinary World)
11. The Resurrection
12. The Return with the Elixir

Departure
Initiation
Return

Seth Barrish's "Universal Story Structure"

Seth Barrish is a Broadway Director in New York City whose credits include Mike Birbiglia's *The New One*. Part of what make Seth so successful is ensuring that his plays follow his "universal story structure."

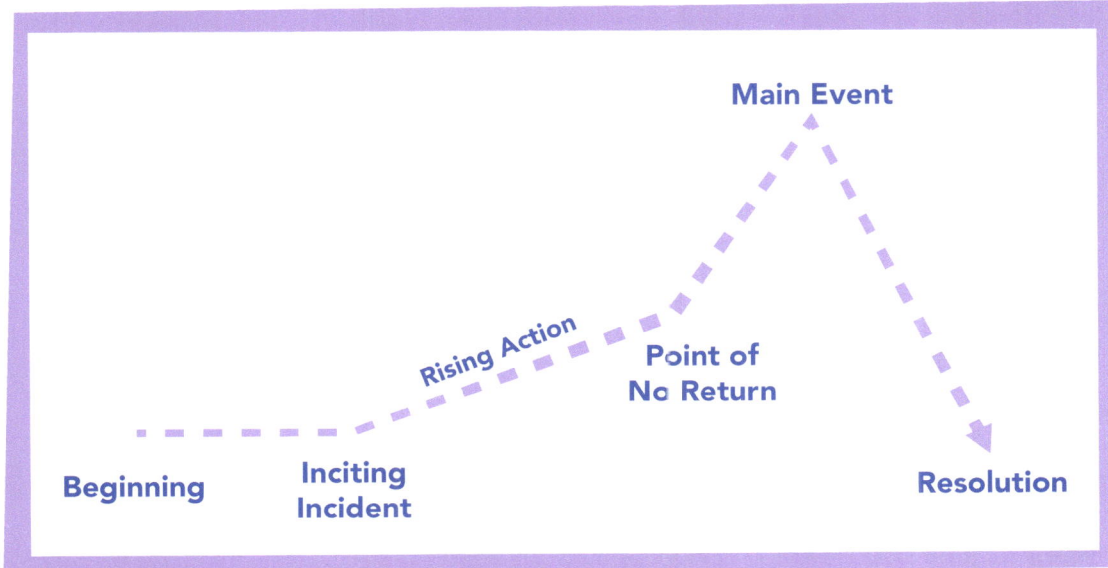

This looks a bit like Freytag's pyramid except skewed off to the side. The major difference here is that the "main event" happens just before the end. One of the nicknames for "the main event" is *the point* of the story because, essentially, this is *why* you're telling this story.

WHAT are the characteristics of a "main event?" How do you recognize it?

One is that they almost always happen right towards the end.

Two is they almost always mark a significant change in the course of action. In other words, something's happened kind of throughout the whole story. When you get to that thing, something very, very different is going on.

Three, there is often a *reveal*...some information that is made known to either the characters or the audience or both.

Four, there is sometimes an extreme physical event, like somebody started sobbing or something gets destroyed or somebody's attacked, or something like that. Not all main events have extreme physical events. Many do.

Five, and this is, to us, a huge identifier... Once you've gotten to the main event, you can now end your story and it's largely the same story. (If whatever follows the main event is essential, you probably aren't at the main event.)

Six, if there's a title, there's often a relationship between the main event and the title.

For example, let's take a look at the story structure of *The Wizard of Oz*. Notice that when we get to the Main Event that it pretty well satisfies all six of those points about main events. In fact, not only does it happen near the end, there are only about 90 seconds left in the film when Dorothy wakes back up in Kansas.

Beginning
Dorothy lives with her Aunt Em and her dog, Toto, on a Kansas farm.

Inciting Incident
Toto bites mean Miss Gulch who takes Toto away, intending to have him put down.

Rising Action
A bunch of dramatic stuff happens, including: Toto escapes, Dorothy takes him and runs away, a tornado comes and transports them to Oz where she has many adventures culminating in finding out "The Wizard" is not actually a wizard at all.

Point of No Return
The hot air balloon leaves without Dorothy. She is stuck in Oz.

Main Event
Glenda the Good Witch returns and tells Dorothy that she has had the power to return all along. All she has to do is click her ruby slippers together and say, "There's no place like home." The big reveal! *She* has the magic! *She* is the true Wizard of Oz!

Resolution
Dorothy and Toto wake up back home in Kansas and she vows never to run away again because there's no place like home!

Find Your Story's Five-Second Moment

Matthew Dicks, in his great book on storytelling, *Storyworthy*, sums it up perfectly:

"There are many secrets to storytelling, but there is one fundamental truth above all others that must be understood before a storyteller can ever be successful:

All great stories — regardless of length or depth or tone — tell the story of a five-second moment in a person's life.

Got that?

Let me say it again: Every great story ever told is essentially about a five-second moment in the life of a human being, and the purpose of the story is to bring that moment to the greatest clarity possible."

This is perfectly in sync with Seth Barrish's "Main Event," and both Barrish and Dicks agree that this "Main Event" or "five-second moment" should happen as close to the end as possible. As Seth says, *"This is the point of your story. Anything after that is superfluous."*

Matthew Dicks is a master of this and it is the secret to why he has won so many Moth SLAM events. These "five-second moments" usually contain a twist, or a "big reveal," and often touch the heart quite profoundly.

As in the story of *The Wizard of Oz*, the main event's big reveal is that Dorothy had the power to return home all along! The guy floating away in the hot air balloon was a fraud.

Dorothy is the *real* Wizard of Oz. Only *she* has the power to transport herself back to Kansas. This is the *point* of the story. So, she clicks her heels together, wakes up back home in Kansas and 90 seconds later the movie is OVER.

Now, apply this to your story

When you are crafting your story, keep the overall arc of the story in mind. Your listener needs this sort of dramatic structure to keep them hooked. Storytelling is not reporting the facts as they happened. You have to elaborate on certain parts and leave other details out. You can even leave whole characters out if their being there is not in service of the story.

Before Launching: Make It Even Better

Once you have a great story polish it up so it sparkles.

Use Sensory Rich Language

Use words and phrases from our five sensory modalities.

As an example, you could use words like these that evoke pictures and images in your listener's mind and make your story shine:

> The emerald city was dazzling.
>
> She was a bright-eyed child.
>
> I was peering into the dark corners of the basement.
>
> She had a flash of inspiration.
>
> From my viewpoint things were looking up.
>
> Karl was green around the gills.
>
> In the deepening shadows of the night.
>
> Bob was lit up like a Christmas tree.

Or you could use the phrases like the following to conjure up the *soundscape* of the moment so it really resonates:

The sound of sizzling bacon called me to the breakfast table.

Sue was barking up the wrong tree.

The call of nature was screeching at full volume.

My confession was met by deafening silence.

Echoes of my footsteps reverberated in the empty hallway.

Eddie marched to the beat of a different drum.

The congregation was howling with laughter in spite of their efforts to keep silent.

On that note, you could use descriptive words like these that connect with the *feel* of an experience so it really hits home:

The kitten felt safe and at home beneath Sam's warm ear.

John hoped his venture would land on solid ground.

I know you'll grab hold of this idea and run with it.

Joshua's heart was heavy when he thought about his loss.

Everyone but the groom could see the bride had itchy feet.

That demotion was just the kick in the butt I needed.

The cowboy was so laid back he was practically sleeping.

If this team can all pull together we'll win this game.

Mary's bold attitude ruffled some feathers around the office.

And, of course, there are words that bring up _smells_ and _tastes_. These really spice things up.

The situation stunk to high heaven.

The fragrance of gardenias wafted through the room.

She was as sweet as cheap candy on Halloween.

He was left with a sour taste in his mouth.

This job was one she could really sink her teeth into.

Proclamation of an Edit by Jacques Clement Wagrez, 1891

Part III
TELLING Your Story

Giving Voice
to Your Story

People have forgotten how to tell a story. Stories don't have a middle or an end any more. They usually have a beginning that never stops beginning.

—Steven Spielberg

Now TELL YOUR TALE OUT LOUD and in front of people

Now that you have either found or written the story you are going to be telling, it's time to bring it to life.

Fortunately, if you've crafted a good story, the tell ng of it gets a whole lot easier. And, when you tell it well, you can make a grocery list sound exciting. Here's how.

The Power of VOICE in Storytelling

This book talks a lot about how to structure and write a story, but let's also remember that when you tell your story out loud, how you use your voice is a key consideration. When we use our voices, we have many options in how we express ourselves.

Here are some of the factors to consider in developing your own storytelling voice

- **Volume and *shifts* of volume**
- **Tone**
- **Rhythm**
- **Use of pauses**
- **Congruity with content**
- **Overall dynamic structure of the delivery**

Let's look at what these mean:

Volume

This may seem basic, but be loud enough to be heard easily and use changes in volume at key moments in your story. The key term here is "changes in volume." If everything is all at one sound level, people can sometimes lose interest. Look to have the volume be congruent with the context. Don't be afraid to go from a roar to a whisper if that's appropriate to the story.

Tone

How you sound in terms of tone will also have a big effect on how well the story is communicated. Different types of voice tone include nasal, deep, round, gritty, and more. Of course, if your story includes different people speaking then you can shift your tonality. When your grandmother from the old country scolded you, let us know what it sounded like.*

(*Note the Word of Caution below)

The bottom line is people want to enjoy the experience of listening to you, so strive to make your voice as pleasant as possible. A good exercise is to listen to radio and TV presenters who earn a living from presenting stories to big audiences and use your voice the same way they do. Record yourself and practice. You might even consider taking voice lessons. It's not just for singing. A good voice coach can really help you improve your presentation skills.

A Word of Caution:
Beware of mimicking or doing accents. If you are going to be telling your story in public, be very wary about using accents or mimicking other people. If your story doesn't work in your own voice or that of your people of origin, it might be best to consider another story. In our experience, imitating accents or mannerisms from another culture rarely works and often offends.

Rhythm

When people listen to a story, the rhythm you use is a key part of getting and maintaining good attention. If there is no change in rhythm, its highly likely you will lose audience attention or put them into a trance. Be careful not to go too fast. Often people rush ahead like some racing commentator and there's barely time to breathe. Which leads us to the use of...

Pauses

One of the hardest skills to master is the ability to pause when telling a story. Pauses allow SPACE and space is a powerful tool for getting and maintaining audience attention.

Congruity with Content

Have the words, phrases, meanings and sounds be congruent with each other. For example, the word "stretch" could be spoken so the sound is "s–t–r–e–t–c–h," rather than in a clipped manner. If you said, "the door slammed shut," you could emphasize that word in a louder voice, like "the door SLAMMED shut."

Overall Dynamic Structure of the Delivery

Just as all great stories have a beginning, middle and an end, each vocal performance of the story should have a *dynamic* structure. This means using all the elements mentioned here in a way that supports the structure. Maybe you'll start slow, talk faster and gesture more in the middle of the story, build to a dramatic peak... (pause) and then slow back down again. There are no hard and fast rules, but the key is to get and maintain audience attention.

It's useful to record yourself delivering a story at different speeds so you hear from a third position how different this is in effect. Of course, the best way to gauge feedback is to present to other live human beings.

Some HOMEPLAY for Your VOICE

Good storytellers have the ability to use their voices in a wide range of expressions. They can be loud as a lion or quiet as a mouse if the story calls for it. Many storytellers make a point of being able to do different voices and different accents very accurately. This much is clear: the more flexibility and control you have over your voice, the better.

ACT as IF

Here's a fun way to practice using your voice in a variety of ways. In this exercise, speak a story out loud and every few sentences radically switch your tone of voice to match how you imagine the person depicted would be speaking. It'll only take a minute or two to progress through the characters listed.

Tell your story as you would if you were...

whispering in a library

A News Anchor on TV

Quietly trying to sell stolen goods from beneath your trench coat...

A SLAM POETRY COMPETITOR

An excited teenager after a first date!

Lessons From a Stand-Up

Never Tell A Boring Story Again

A stand-up comic gets up on stage, tells a story about buying peaches at the grocery store and makes everyone in the place go into hysterics. Then your average Joe gets up on stage at an open mic night and wonders why his "incredibly funny" joke fell flat. What's up with that?

That's because seasoned veterans know the reality of stand-up comedy... it's not the story that is important, but rather, how it's told.

Lucky for you, we have the...

Seven Keys to Telling a Story Like a Stand-Up

1. Keep it Tight

The first rule of comedy is to be brief and to get to the first laugh as quickly as possible. In storytelling, that means you should have a strong opening line. Hitting the ground running like that will draw your listeners in and they'll be more likely to stay invested if the story hits any flat points. Delete anything from the story, even entire characters, that you don't absolutely need. Keep it lean. Only use descriptives when they're necessary and, when you do use them, use good ones. Don't use "little" when "miniature" or "teensy–weensy" are so much more interesting.

2. Embellish Select Details

Stand-up comics embellish certain details IF it helps make the story (joke) more funny or engaging, and leave other details out. As an example, if the character in your joke is large, make them enormous, like a balloon in Macy's Thanksgiving Day Parade.

3. Use Story Twists

An unwritten rule (until now) that most stand-ups observe is that there should be a laugh about every eight seconds or so. I'm NOT saying that your story should be riddled with punch lines because it will cease being believable, but that there should be enough to keep the audience engaged and listening carefully. So instead of saying, "...this lady had a Siamese cat," include a humorous detail about the cat. Like "...this cat didn't just walk across the floor, she sauntered like Michelle Pfeiffer playing Catwoman."

4. Work the Crowd

Have you ever thought a stand-up was a genius because she asked a question to the audience and then was so able to riff hilariously off their answers? Maybe it was genius, of maybe it was more like she asked leading questions like, "Does anybody here have a pet?" And then when she sees somebody in the third row laughing and nodding asks, "Do you ever wonder what they're thinking?" And then the comic launches into the very joke she was going to tell in the first place. Asking questions of the audience keeps them engaged and they'll be more personally involved in the story.

5. Act Out the Characters

Sometimes you can enhance a story by acting out and even exaggerating a character's mannerisms a little bit.

Of course, as we stated in the warning a few pages ago, be very careful when imitating other people. Be respectful and don't make fun of anyone or any groups unless it's the group you inhabit personally. It won't help your story and can come across as offensive.

6. Practice

You know that old joke... The tourist in New York City stops a cop and asks, "How to you get to Carnegie Hall?" The cop says, "Practice."

Telling a story like a stand-up takes practice and you can bet that a good one will have honed his or her routine for many hours before it's ready for prime time. Even the best stand-up comics continue to go to open mic nights to try out new material and stay fresh.

Tell your story as often as you can. Tell it at parties, tell it to your cat, tell it into your phone and listen back to the recording. It's amazing how much you learn when you test it out in front of people, even just one person. Your performance night should not be the first time you've told the story.

7. Have a Good Ending

Stand-up comics strive to end on the biggest laugh. Since listeners tend to remember only the beginning and the last part of an act or a story, it's good to have a big finish. Leave them wanting more.

Performing Your Story

" Your story must reflect change over time. A story cannot simply be a series of remarkable events. You must start out as one version of yourself and end as something new. **"**

—Matthew Dicks

Manage Your State

(...and always have fun)

Did you ever have one of those days when everything was flowing? Where you seemed to just be at your best and you were "on?" You were witty, you were energized, people responded well to you and things just went your way?

Or – have your ever had the opposite sort of day, where everything seemed stacked against you and nothing seemed to work out?

While it may feel like the kind of day we are having is due to people and events outside of ourselves, most of the time this has more to do with us and the way we are being that day. Because when you are in a great state of mind, you tend to do great things and if something happens you respond resourcefully. Conversely, when you are in a foul state of mind (angry or sad or depressed) you tend to do less-than-great things, and if something happens you might react badly.

Fortunately, there are things we can do about that and in this section of the book, we're going to show you some of the best ways.

Essentially, it boils down to this: Your state of mind (your mood) is created by two major factors.

1. **What you are thinking about and focusing on in your mind.**

2. **How you are using your body and facial expressions.**

So if you are thinking about happy things and are using your body and facial expressions in a like fashion, you'll feel happy. And, if you are focusing more on bad things and are using your body and face in ways that express that, you'll feel bad.

Therefore, if you want to feel a certain way, focus on thoughts that will lead you there and act as if you are, and you will be soon enough.

Does this sound a bit crazy? Hear us out. Please, read on...

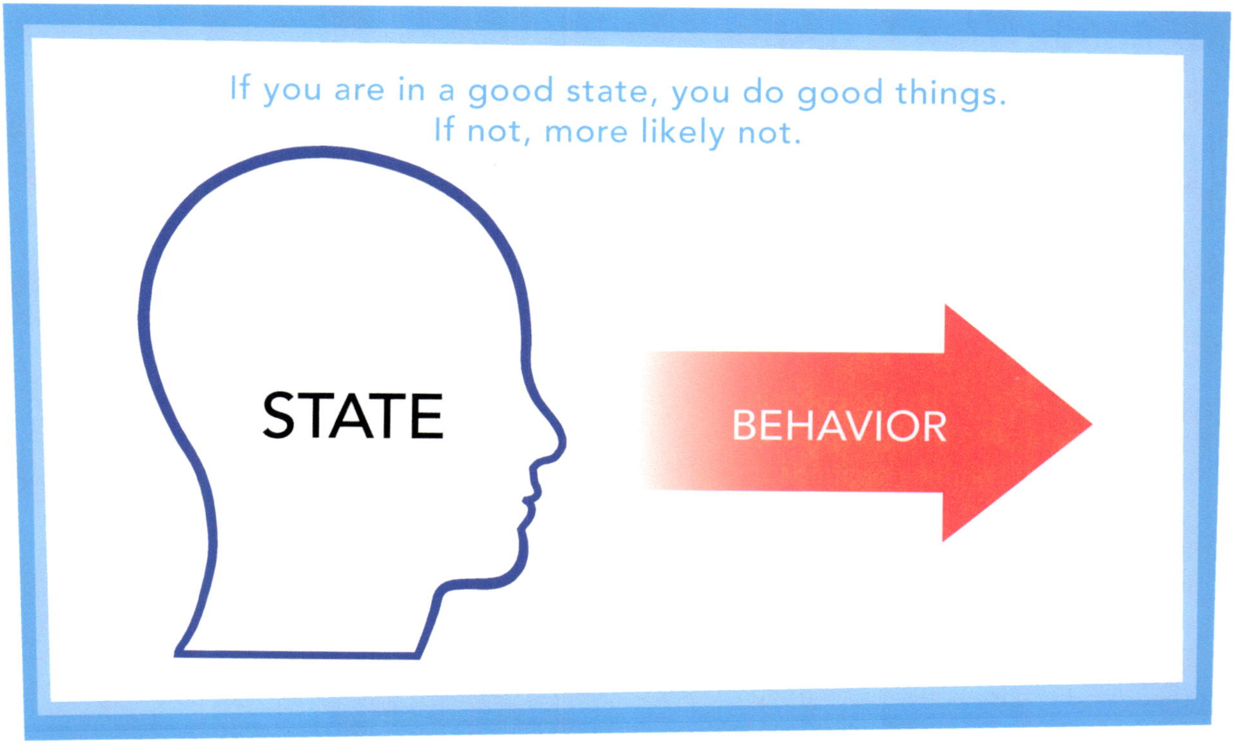

If you are in a good state, you do good things.
If not, more likely not.

STATE

BEHAVIOR

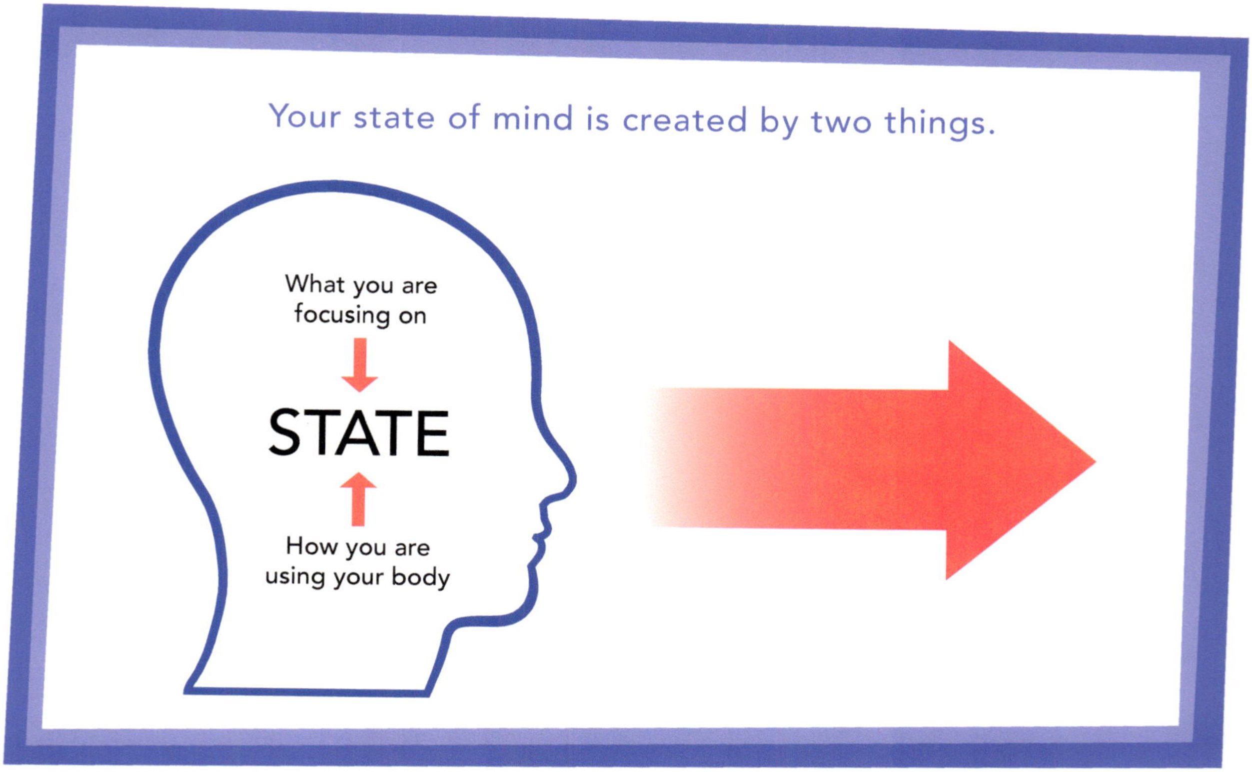

Your state of mind is created by two things.

What you are
focusing on

STATE

How you are
using your body

How Does Your Physiology Affect How You Feel?

More and more science is showing that our body posture and facial expression *directly* influence our state of mind. Many go so far as to say your body posture and facial expression actually *create* your state; that without using your body and face you wouldn't feel the emotion.

TRY THIS EXPERIMENT

If you are physically able to do so right now, stand up and stand the way you'd be standing if you were sad and depressed.

Really. Try it.

Stop reading. Put the book down and do it. Simply stand the way you'd be standing if you were sad and depressed. Then come back and read some more. We'll wait...

Short Intermission

Welcome back.

What you may have noticed is that you did what every human being on the planet does; that to feel sad and depressed, you must look downward, breathe shallowly, tilt your head down, maybe lean your weight to one side.

This is what a human MUST DO to feel so poorly.

Now, try this on for size...

Stand up again, but bounce up and down of your toes, take deep breaths, put your shoulders back, look up at the ceiling and put a huge smile on your face. Now try to be sad and depressed using *this* physiology.

You will find this an impossible task. You can't feel depressed like that.

It's true. Studies have shown that if people artificially tighten their smile muscles, they feel happier, and vice versa.

You've probably seen that Ted Talk on Power Poses. Same thing.

The Cape Walk

Your imagination can give you superpowers.

Because your physiology is such an enormous factor in your psychological state, it's nice to know that there is a really easy thing you can do to feel great. Or at least as good as possible. The "Cape Walk" is crazy simple and amazingly effective.

How to do it

First, let's get a baseline for comparison. Stand up and just walk around the room you're in for about a minute. Just notice how you are walking, how you are using your body, how you relate to the space you are in.

Second, stop and close your eyes. Now imagine that you have a cape on your back. It's a cape like Superman's cape or Wonder Woman's cape, or a queen's or a king's and now, it's YOURS. You OWN it. Feel the power.

Now, open your eyes and walk around the room again while wearing the cape. Notice the difference. Feel how your posture is different. How you are breathing differently. Notice how your move differently and how you own the space you are in in a very different way.

WEAR YOUR CAPE whenever you want to feel more power and confidence.

SO - Your Physiology is Half of the Equation - What's the Other Half?

What you are focusing on in your mind. Of course, you probably already knew that. It is pretty obvious when you think about it. But did you know that it is remarkably easy to change that?

We will show you how in the next few pages to come, but first, let's try another experiment.

TRY THIS EXPERIMENT

We want to test your skills of observation. So just stop what you're doing for a minute, look around you and answer this question: What can you notice within your surroundings and including your own garments, that is made out of metal? Take 30 seconds and see how much you can notice that you hadn't noticed before. Imagine you will win a large cash prize if you succeed in naming everything metal around you.

Now for the test: Close your eyes and list everything that is blue.

You will notice that you have missed many of the blue things that surround you, maybe even your own clothing. Why? Because your brain was doing its job. You asked it to notice metal things and it did. But it missed out on all the blue things, not to mention the red things, yellow things, plastic things, etc.

Your brain is a question answering machine and whatever question you ask it, it will seek an answer for.

Good Questions versus Bad Questions

Imagine you are about to go out on stage to tell your story. Imagine that you can't seem to stop worrying about the same question: "What if I mess up? What if I forget my story?" How do you think you'd feel? We know we'd be worried and stressed because our brains would be playing images of the answers to those questions. We'd see ourselves messing up and being ridiculed by the cruel audience until we slunk off the stage with our tail between our legs.

But what if, instead, you asked yourself questions like "How great is this? How can I best have fun doing this? I wonder what I should have for dinner later?"

You brain's job is to seek the answer it has been asked. So ask it good questions. When you combine the positive focus of your attention with positive physiology, you will be in a good state to have fun being wonderful.

Self Talk and Asking Good Questions

Some examples:

1. What is/was great about this story/experience?
2. What did I learn? (or What can I learn here, now?)
3. What is not perfect yet?
4. How can I go about making it better while being gentle with myself?
5. How can I enjoy (have FUN) doing the things necessary to make it the way I want it?
6. What would (insert mentor here) do? How would (he or she) make this better?

Use Your Body... or Not

Some storytellers use their bodies a lot. They move around, they gesticulate, they virtually act out the story. That's fine. If you're really good at that, then let that be part of your style.

AND... you don't have to. Many storytellers stand relatively still and rely on their voice and the imagery in the story to make it visually interesting to the listener.

There is not a right way or a wrong way to approach this. You'll find your own style.
The most important thing is for you to *be comfortable* up there when you are telling your story.
Wear your cape. Have FUN.

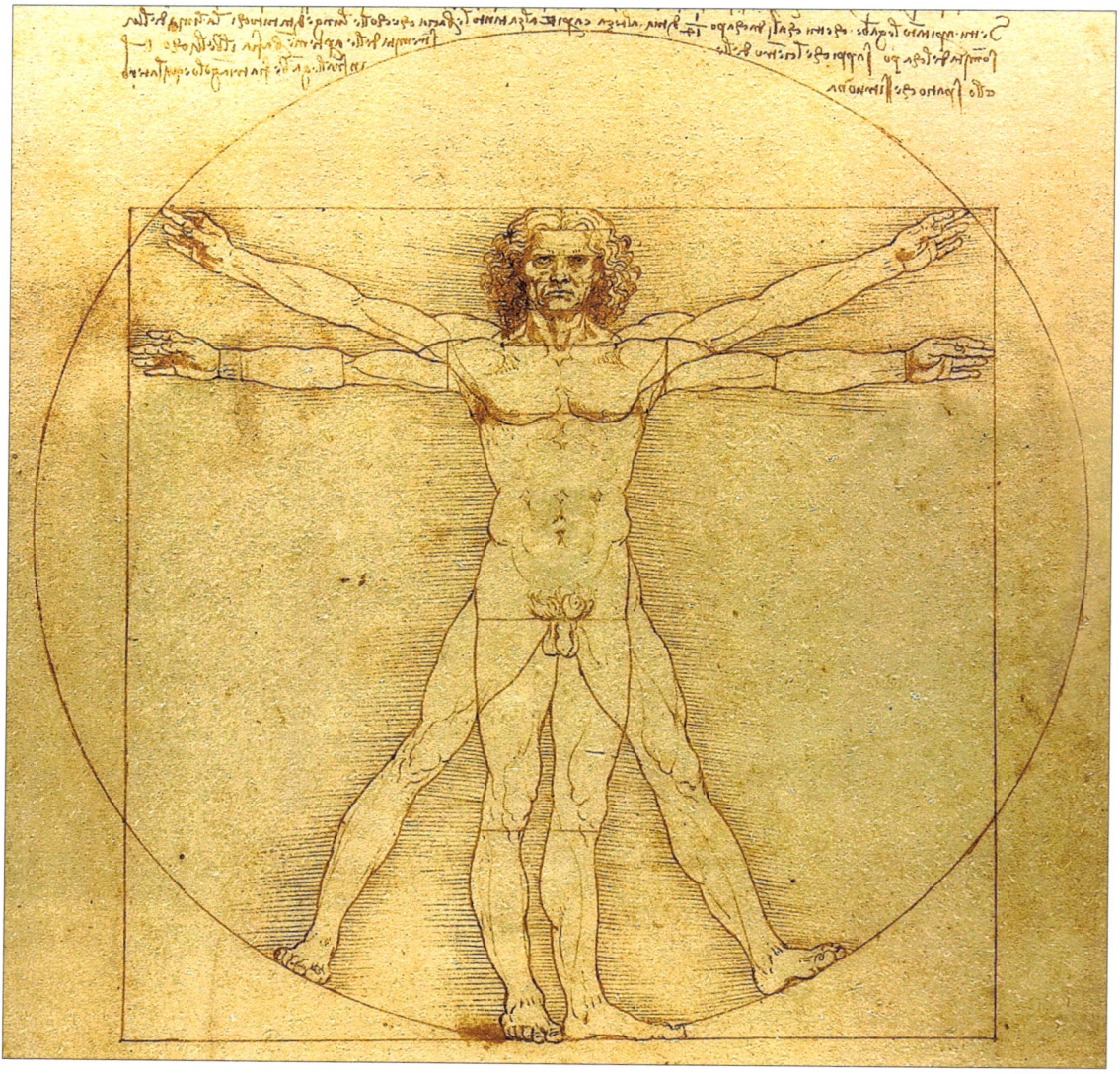

Bottom Line

Have fun. Think of your storytelling less like a performance and more like a conversation between you and your closest friend. Trust your practice. Be comfortable. Be yourself. Have fun telling your story.

Let me tell you a story that is pertinent in this regard from my own life. It involves piano playing, not storytelling, but the effect is the same.

As this story unfolds I am twenty-three years old.

I am in the green room of the recital hall at SUNY Fredonia in upstate New York, waiting to go on to play my final solo concert in college.

I have spent the last five years of my life getting through a four-year college program as a piano major – not because I was slow, but because I had added an extra year to study at a conservatory in London.

I needed to.

My freshman year was a train wreck. I hadn't been ready for the demands of a music conservatory and very nearly got asked to leave. One teacher in particular lobbied for my dismissal and I survived by the skin of my teeth.

Over the next three years I'd slogged my way back up into the good graces of most of the faculty by a lot of hard work and toeing the line.

The added year abroad had helped my playing immensely but now there is still one more test to pass. It is the hardest test of all for a music major... the juried senior recital. I have to play a public recital that will be judged by a jury of four faculty members.

And, of course, this jury includes that one professor who, I know, wants and expects me to fail.

He still thinks I should never have been given a second chance and is looking forward to proving he was right.

In preparation for this recital I've been practicing like never before.

I've spent hours upon hours in the practice room, playing the pieces over and over again, trying to get the hard parts right.

Then I had a lesson with my wonderful piano teacher, Mr. T. Richard Patterson. He's a great teacher and was employing some unusual methods to keep me on my toes leading up to the recital. While I was playing he was crawling around on the floor, trying to distract me, forcing me to focus. He took out a pencil and wrote on the walls, mumbled something and then erased it. And then, at the end of the lesson, he looked at me with an extremely serious look on his face, slowly shook his head and said, "Well. I don't know, Douglas P., (His nickname for me. I never knew what it meant.) I don't know if you'll make it. Some of it is ok but there's still an awfully long way to go."

So I went running back to the practice room to do a few more hours of practice.

And now here we are. Finally. The day of the concert.

Students, teachers, friends, and family are assembling in the concert hall to bear witness to this event.

I'm so nervous I'm jumping out of my skin, and pacing back and forth in the green room.

Mr. Patterson knocks on the door and I open it to let him in. I fully expect the same, worried expression on his face I saw two days ago, but I'm wrong. It's like he's been drinking... smiling, relaxed and kinda goofy. He's like a different person. I want to shake him and say, "Who are you and what have you done to Mr. Patterson?" I've never seen him so loose. He's smiling from ear to ear like a kid with a gift certificate in a toy store.

He stands squarely in front of me, reaches up to straighten my tie and quietly says, "You've done the work. You're ready. Trust me. Just go out there and have *fun*."

He shakes my hand, turns, and walks out.

A portrait of the Author as a young man

Part IV
USING Your Story

Applications

" The most powerful person in the world is the storyteller. The storyteller sets the vision, values, and agenda of an entire generation that is to come. "

—Steve Jobs

Different, practical uses of stories

There are many, many situations where good storytelling gives you great benefits. Here are just a few specific applications and some key points to do it right.

1. MAKING A WEDDING TOAST

Toast-don't roast

2. TELLING STORIES IN BUSINESS

The ART of Motivating, Promoting Teamwork, and so much more!

3. TELLING STORIES IN COACHING

Teaching Tales and The ART of Therapeutic Metaphor

First up:

Roman coin depicting the adlocutio, *an emperor's motivational address to the soldiers*

How to do a WEDDING TOAST

Congratulations! You've been asked to give a toast at a wedding! That's a really nice thing and an honor you should feel very good about it, indeed. And it is also a special situation with its own unique concerns to be mindful of. Because even if you are used to public speaking, this can be a tough crowd; a wedding brings together people who might not know each other, who may come from very different backgrounds and may span a wide spectrum of attitudes and beliefs. So mind your step. Avoid the temptation to wow the crowd with your best stand–up routine and be content with having your contribution be pleasant and a bit heartwarming. Keep it family friendly, appropriate for the new in-laws and, perhaps most importantly, keep it short and sweet. Most people are far more interested in getting to the open bar and dance floor than in listening to a long speech.

That being said, many of the same elements that go into any good story telling apply here as well, and here are some tried and true tips and guidelines you can use to craft your own winning toast.

Four Do's and a Don'ts for a Great Toast

1. DO keep inside jokes to a minimum. The toast is *about* the couple getting married but *for* everybody else.

2. DO give a shout-out to family VIPs – like extremely old relatives or someone who has traveled an especially long distance to be there, etc.

3. DO be flattering – even if you have to work at it. Like, if the bride is a hard partier, compliment her on her *joie de vivre*. If the groom is boring, say he's down to earth. You get the idea.

4. DO strive for balance. Some light, good–natured humor is fine and it's good to end on some heartfelt sentiment, just not too much of either. Aim to leave everyone with a good feeling.

And finally here's the big don't...
5. DON'T talk about past misbehavior or past relationships. This is the wedding, not the bachelor party or bridal shower. Trust me on this one.

A Toast Template (Note the short and sweetness)

(Please note: Depending on your specific situation be sure to be aware of appropriate pronoun use. Check with the wedding party in advance.)

It's a great joy to be here with so many great friends and family, to celebrate the joining together of [the couple's names]. *It's wonderful to have with us...* [Give a shout-out to family VIPs here (see tip 2 above)]

I first met [the member of the wedding party you are representing] *at* [wherever you met him or her]. *I knew immediately that s/he was* [genuine compliment about them as a person]. *Since then, we've known each other through* [list some of the things you've done together - school, clubs, teams, jobs, etc. Finish up with a brief anecdote of something you did together that exemplifies their fine character].

But life really began to change for [him or her] *when s/he met* [spouse to be]. *With* [spouse's] *amazing* [list a few good qualities], *it was clear to everyone that s/he had found someone special. We always knew s/he was a great* [woman/guy], *but* [spouse] *brought out the best in* [her/him]. [Illustrate with an example if possible].

[If you can remember your friend telling you anything about wanting to get serious with this person or a time when you noticed your friend changing for the better thanks to the new partner, mention it here for a nice tug at the heartstrings.]

[Next, if you have any funny but *safe* anecdotes about your friend getting adjusted to coupledom, throw them in. For an easy laugh, you could warn the spouse about some bad habit of your friend. Keep it light and family–friendly.]

So I couldn't be happier that my friend has met such a great partner, and that they're embarking on a new life together. Let's all raise our glasses to many years of happiness to come. Cheers!

Delivering Your Toast

If you find yourself in the position of having to give a toast, whether at a wedding or some other occasion, the most important preparation is to practice it out loud to another human being. Get someone— they don't have to be a storytelling coach— and say, "Hey, I've got to do a toast for the wedding and I need to practice it. Got a minute to let me try it out on you?"

The thing about getting the thoughts out of your head, speaking them aloud and having them witnessed by another human being is, to some extent, the wisdom the listener imparts by simply being on the receiving side.

Other practice is fine as well: like driving to the wedding and speaking into the rear view mirror, but there's nothing better than saying it out loud to another human being. Just getting it out of your mouth two or three times, and getting a little bit

of reaction to it, works wonders. Stories exist between people. Don't wait till you're standing up at the wedding reception with a microphone in your hand for that to be the first time that that story is between you and another person.

One more thing... A lot of the key to the success in delivering a toast is to be grounded and confident. And the secret to feeling confident when delivering a toast is the same as the secret to improv (*Improv, or Improvisational theatre, is the form of theatre, often comedy, in which most or all of what is performed is unplanned or unscripted and made up on the spot*).

The secret to improv is that a lot of the pleasure, and even the laughter, in improv is that the audience understands that you're walking a tightrope without a net. They are fully aware that you don't know what's coming next and that you're making it up as you go along. So when that underlying tension in the audience is released, it is pleasurable and often funny.

It's a similar dynamic when a non–professional needs to speak in front of a group. So when you get up to deliver your toast, stand like you are the most confident person in the world, make sure you're breathing in a way that sends a message to your body "I'm calm here; everything's okay," and maybe even find some enjoyment of the moment. The audience will carry you. You will be OK.

Next we look at:

Telling Stories in Business

The ART of Motivation and so much more!

Here's the secret to using stories in business: *Business people are people, too.*

ALL people respond to stories because stories are message delivery systems that human beings are wired to listen to. When you learn to tell your business–related story in a dynamic way with a dramatic narrative, you'll connect with people on a deep level, your message will stick with them, and you will be more persuasive.

And if we are talking about marketing, then good heavens! MARKETING *IS* STORIES! I'm sure you can relate to that. In this section of the book we're talking more about using stories in management situations or within the corporate environment in general.

Hold on now... Stories? In Business?

Yes. Absolutely. But don't take my word for it. Let's ask **Josh Broder**, story coach to the stars. Josh has shared his storytelling wisdom with corporations from Apple to Nike and everything in between.

I sat down with him and asked him, "How do you teach the use of stories in business?" This page and the next page is what I learned from him. Not surprisingly, he started with a story...

The Most Powerful Teaching Story for Business

Imagine that you have a business–oriented message you want to get across and you begin your presentation like this:

"I was standing on the high diving board, looking down at the water far below me. I've never seen water that far away. I've never been on a high board that high. I was looking down at my adorable girlfriend in her adorable bikini; she was looking up at me waiting to see me dive off the high diving board for the very first time."
If your business oriented message starts like that, in my experience, you're going to get listening out of folks. They're actually hanging on what you're going to say.

Crafting your own Personal Business Teaching Story

So how does a businessperson take their corporate message up on the diving board? You create it backwards. You start by getting clear about what is the idea or teaching point that you want to get across and then you seek a story from your own personal history that will illustrate that message. This is because the most powerful teaching stories for business are stories about *yourself* and the best person to tell your story is *you*.

Sometimes the process of finding the right story takes some time. That's OK. Take all the time you need.

Once you settle on a good story that could work to get that message across, you come up with at least three teaching points that could be taken from your story. Usually stories hold multiple teaching points, and like a good screenplay for a movie, if something gets said or happens in that movie, it's there for a reason. It has to move the story along. So we do a lot of editing and revising. Things get added. Things get removed.

Then you structure your story by deciding on the setting. Where does this story take place? You want your listener or listeners to start to see the movie of the story in their minds and you evoke those images with language. It doesn't have to be seven coats of thick paint of sensory details, but what are those two or three or four things that will do the job? What's the quality of the light, what's the temperature, what are you holding in your hands?

So, like the story about being on the diving board, looking down at the water far below, you don't have to describe every single detail about the community swimming pool but hopefully everyone projects whatever "girlfriend in adorable bikini" means to them.

Then, within that setting, you create a situation for which the stakes are very high for that person at that moment. The stakes may not be as high as birth of a child or the death of a loved one, but for that kid at that moment, diving off the high diving board for the first time, that was a lot more real than anything else you could imagine.

And usually, in the story, there is a moment of realization for the character. And because it's business and we don't want anybody to miss the point, the meaning of that transformation is pretty explicitly pointed out. We want to make sure the listener gets it and that all the members of the business team we're talking to take away the same message.

Sometimes a storyteller might be resistant to really put the button on the story like that, because they are afraid they might come off as condescending if they spell it out (and in other settings, they would be right.) But in business you need the button. Because when you've really crafted your story well and everything is in service of that teaching point, there's a beautiful moment when the audience goes "Ah, yes! I get it," and you see that story getting deposited deep.

One marker of its success is when that story becomes the metaphoric language of your team. You know? So you tell a story to your team, and then six months later, two guys who heard the story are talking, and one turns to the other and says "don't climb that diving board until you're sure you want to jump off." When you experience that, it's like "whoa."

"There are the events in our lives and then there are the stories we craft from them."
– Josh Broder

The Three Main Story Plots

According to Chip and Dan Heath, authors of the book *Made to Stick,* there are really only three types of stories in all of history.

That level of reductionism is probably inaccurate, but it is undeniably true that most stories you'll hear in the corporate realm will be one of these three types. And, of course, the number one key to making an idea "sticky" is to tell it as a story. Stories encourage a kind of mental simulation or reenactment on the part of the listener that burns the idea into the mind. For example, a flight simulator is much more effective than flash cards in training a pilot.

Here are the three major types of stories the authors delineate:

1. The Challenge Plot

This is the classic underdog, rags to riches, or sheer willpower triumphing over adversity. The key element of the Challenge Plot is that the obstacles seem daunting to the protagonists.

There are literally thousands of examples of this plot. You can probably think of one off the top of your head faster than you can read our example, but here it is: In the 2007 British film, "Run Fatboy Run," we meet an ordinary man named Dennis who works a meaningless job as a security guard in a London dress shop. We learn that five years earlier as a nervous bridegroom, he left his pregnant girlfriend, Libby, at the altar. Now he realizes he made a big mistake and wants to win her back. Unfortunately, Libby is involved with a handsome, attentive, and fit financier who plans to run in a charity marathon. Out-of-shape Dennis enters the race – hoping to impress Libby – even though he only has three weeks to prepare. After much hardship and even a painful injury during the race (when he is deliberately tripped by his rival), he pushes through, prevails against all odds and, of course, gets the girl back.

2. The Connection Plot

A story about people who develop a relationship that bridges a gap – racial, class, ethnic, religious, demographic, or otherwise. For example, the Mean Joe Creene commercial of the 1970s where he makes friends with a scrawny young white kid. All Connection Plots inspire us in social ways. They make us want to help others, be more tolerant of others, work with others, love others.

For an example we need look no further than our man Aesop and the fable of *The Lion and the Mouse:*

A lion lay asleep in the forest, his great head resting on his paws. A timid little mouse came upon him unexpectedly, and in her fright and haste to get away, ran across the lion's nose. Roused from his nap, the lion laid his huge paw angrily on the tiny

creature to kill her. "Spare me!" begged the poor mouse. "Please let me go and some day I will surely repay you."

The lion was much amused to think that a mouse could ever help him. But he was generous and finally let the mouse go.

Some days later, while stalking his prey in the forest, the lion was caught in the coils of a hunter's net. Unable to free himself, he filled the forest with his angry roaring. The mouse knew the voice and quickly found the lion struggling in the net. Running to one of the great ropes that bound him, she gnawed it until it parted, and soon the lion was free.

The lion and the mouse were the unlikeliest of friends forevermore.

3. The Creativity Plot

This involves someone making a mental breakthrough, solving a long-standing puzzle, or attacking a problem in an innovative way.

The movie "Moneyball," based on a book by Michael Lewis, is the story of Billy Beane, general manager of an American professional baseball team. Faced with a tight budget, Beane must reinvent his team by outsmarting the richer ball clubs. Joining forces with Ivy League graduate Peter Brand, Beane builds a team of undervalued talent by taking a sophisticated, computerized approach towards scouting and analyzing players.

Final Word of Advice: Tell Your *Own* Story

The above examples of the three main story plots are only *examples* of the type of plots we're talking about. We are not recommending that you use these stories or really, *any* other stories you may have heard in the past. Even if you think they are just the perfect story to get your point across. Don't tell Colonel Sander's story, tell YOUR story.

It is *much better*, perhaps even critical, to tell stories from your own personal life experiences… especially if you're using these stories to promote your business. Think about it. If you are telling a "Creativity Plot" story to a group of people, wouldn't it be awesome if the creativity being spotlighted in the story was YOUR company's unique out-of-the-box thinking? If you are telling an inspiring "Challenge Plot" story about a person who overcame terrible odds to succeed, wouldn't it be good if that inspiring person was your company's founder?

Now let's look at:

Telling Stories in Coaching

Teaching Tales and The ART of *Therapeutic Metaphor*

Using stories in coaching and therapy is, on one level, very similar to using stories in business in that you want to get a message across to your listener – in this case your client – in a way that will engage their whole brain, including their emotions, and thus be remembered and persuasive. So many of the lessons from the above section can also be applied in coaching.

Of course, the term "coaching" covers a lot of territory. You can be an athletic coach to individual competitors or to teams. You can be a "Life Coach" and help bring out the best in an individual. You can be, for all intents and purposes, a therapist who employs skills and techniques beyond the normal scope of therapy. No matter your specific form of coaching, storytelling has a vital place in your tool kit.

The Magic of the Anecdote

Coaching is often quite spontaneous and there's no time to prepare or practice a longer story – not even a one or two-minute story. After all, you are engaged in a conversation with a person in real time, here and now, present moment stuff. You don't have time to ponder how to come up with your best possible, beautifully scripted story. You've got a few precious seconds to say, "That reminds me of a story…" and start talking.

So there are exactly two things you can do about this:

1. Know a lot of stories.
2. Know how to make up your own stories on the spot that fit the bill.

1: Know a Lot of Stories

You'll want to have some standard stories in your back pocket for typical coaching situations. Stories about things like believing in yourself, persisting, having faith in the process, seeing the bright side, etc. Your stories can come from a movie you saw or a book you read. Stories can be from a TV show or a joke you heard. Children's books can be an excellent source of stories because these are very often simple stories with a moral teaching. You can tell stories you've heard other coaches or seminar leaders tell, you can relate Bible stories or Aesop's fables – the list is endless.

Here is a very short list of the sort of thing I'm talking about.
(The fleshed out stories are easily found through an online search)

- Persistence: Edison failed 1,000 times before succeeding with the light bulb.
- Time Management: The professor and jar of rocks, sand, and water (from Steven Covey).
- Perspective: Guy on the subway car and his kids misbehaving (also from Steven Covey).
- Willingness to work hard: Lance Armstrong and bike riding (yes, I know he also cheated).
- Breaking through barriers: Roger Bannister and the 4–minute mile.
- Going on in spite of disappointing feedback: The poem attributed to Mother Theresa (actually written by Kent M. Keith) called "Do it Anyway."
- Being your best at all times: Carlos Castaneda and Don Juan walking when the boulder falls.
- Humor in face of adversity: The joke with the guy hanging from a cliff when God tells him to let go: "Is anybody else up there?"
- Higher purpose in our jobs: Marianne Williamson saying, "Every job is a front for a church."

Be a Collector of Stories

When you hear a good story, file it away in your memory banks. Copy it into a folder marked "Stories" on your hard drive. Tell it to other people. Practice saying it out loud when you go for your morning walk or while driving to work. Imagine where and with whom you'd be likely to use it with positive effect. Put it in a shoebox.

Buy story collections of inspirational stories or therapeutic metaphors. Read them. Enjoy them. Listen to storytellers. Listen to motivational speakers. Listen to TED talks. (Don't try and memorize what they say, paraphrase and make them your own.)

Then, when you are in conversation with your coaching client, trust your unconscious mind to bring them to mind when appropriate. The famous phrase "that reminds me of a story" is said because the person who said that *was* reminded of a story. That will be you when you let yourself BE a collector of stories.

Use Your Own Life Stories

As a coach or therapist you have a lot of experience, both of your own life and from your work with earlier clients. This is a gold mine of material for stories. The great hypnotherapist/psychotherapist Milton Erickson, M.D., often told stories that started with "I had a client once who…" Of course, you don't mention any names nor cross any boundaries of privacy, but it is great source material for you to illustrate to your current client the point you are trying to get across. AND – your current client does not need to know if your story is 100% factual, nor does it need to be. It's a teaching tale. The purpose of the story is not to reminisce about a moment in history; it is to convey a lesson. So you leave parts out, enhance other parts, craft your story so your client comes away with the life lesson they need to hear clearly in their mind.

Quite a collection: Trinity College Library, Dublin

2: Create Your Own Story from Whole Cloth

The Theraputic Metaphor

To create your own therapeutic metaphor follow this simple process:

1. Listen to your client relate to you their current situation and challenge.

2. Imagine what resource(s)/ understanding(s) they need to get from where they are now to where they want to be

3. Ask your self, "What is this like?"

4. Make up a story with made-up people or animals or objects who enact the analogous solution to the problem.

Here's an example.

Let's say you have a client named Felix whom you've been coaching. Imagine:

1. Felix tells you (or you notice) that he is having trouble getting ahead in life because he has a deep–seated belief that he's not worthy of success.

2. You establish that Felix needs belief in himself and determination to get over that hurdle and succeed.

3. You ask yourself, "What is that like?"

4. You think of dozens of possible scenarios but tell your client:

Hmong story cloth depicting the folktale of Ntxawm *and the Tiger*

"That reminds me of a story. Back in my hometown there was young boy who wanted to be a basketball player his whole life, but everyone thought he was too short. All his life the other kids had made fun of him for being too short to play basketball. So he practiced all by himself. When all the other kids had gone home, he stayed behind and practiced shooting, especially from the free throw line. Always imagining he would hit the game–winning shot at the buzzer.

When it came to try out for the high school team he didn't make the roster, but the coach let him stay on as the team manager. He liked the kid's positive attitude. He went to practice every day and helped set up and clean up after.

Then one day there was a bad flu epidemic and practically the whole team got sick, just before last game of the season. A game that, if they won, would send them to the championship. The coach told him to suit up, because without him there would be only four players and the team would have to forfeit.

He was a mix of excitement and terror when the game started. It was all so sudden. And a first it didn't go very well. The opposing team went up by ten points.

But he and the rest of the team fought back and he started shooting the lights out of the place. It seemed like he couldn't miss. They pulled within just a couple of points with just a few seconds to go and as he was getting ready to shoot to win, he was fouled by one of the other teams' players and his shot missed. But because the referee called the foul, he had two free throws.

So there he was, just as he had always imagined it. Two free throws to win the game. He was so nervous he was shaking. This was *not* how he imagined it. The ref handed him the ball and he took a few deep breaths to try and steady himself.

He took his first shot and it bounced up off the rim, once, twice, and then rolled around the rim before it fell in. Tie game! One more point to go! He was going to do it!

The ref handed him the ball, he took another few deep breaths... bounced the ball three times, just like he always did... then finally, he shoots. The ball bounces high off the rim and misses! He missed!

But, before anyone could react, he streaked like lightning towards the hoop, leapt up high in the air, snagged the ball out of the hands of the opposing center and tipped the ball into the basket! The team won by two points! No one ever forgot how the short kid out–jumped everybody to win that game and send the team to the championship."

Remember this is a made-up story. It is the form of it that counts, not the gender of the protagonist or the details of the plot. That is all made up out of whole cloth and can change while you are telling it.

In the story above it could be a virtually identical story but the kid is playing baseball instead of basketball and is too tall instead of too short. Or the story might find our hero wanting to compete in the bobsled but is too fat, or too slow. Or it's about a young girl. Or it's about an older person in their new job at a startup company. Or it's about a dog that's new at his/her job guarding the sheep. Or it's about a black sheep when all the other sheep are white. Or it's about Rudolph the Reindeer with his shiny red nose. Or it's about a chesspiece pawn who puts the opposing King in checkmate and how she feels about that. Or it's about a car who wins a street race. Or who loses a street race but transports an injured person to the hospital on time.

It literally could be about anything as long as the protagonist draws upon their inner strength to overcome an obstacle and achieve victory by never giving up and exceeding the expectation of others, because that's the lesson Felix needs to learn.

The Therapeutic Metaphor Illustrated

Your client situation can be graphed like this.

A: Where they are now mentally, emotionally and behaviorally; their current situation or "state."

C: Where they want to get to, or their "desired state."

?: The Missing Piece. They don't how to get from A to C.

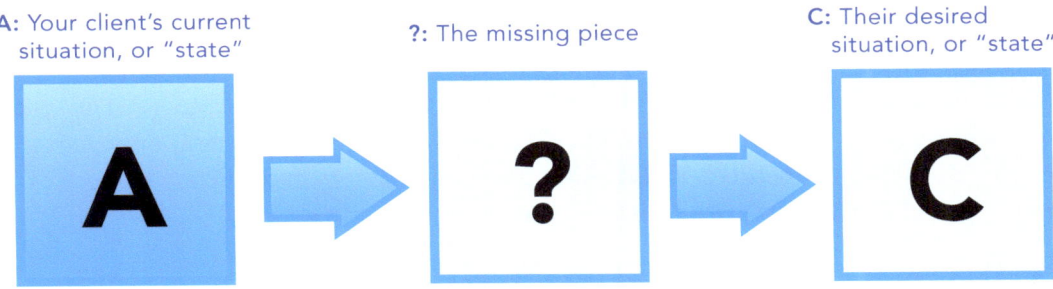

So you ask yourself, *what is that like?* and think of analogous situations.

Y ou take the people, places, and situation that your client describes to you and imagine what that could be like and create an analogous situation that's *like* your client's situation, only different.

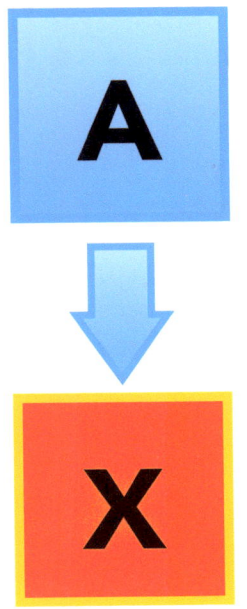

Then come up with a story that describes a metaphorical solution to the client's problem within that analogous situation.

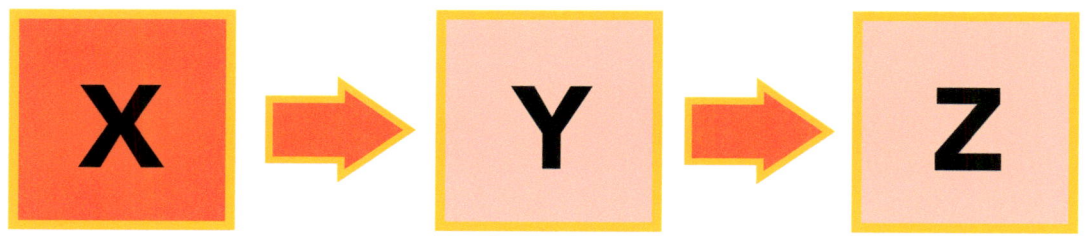

In business, you might be prone to telling your listeners the "moral to the story," *à la* Aesop's fables. That's fine. Business people need that directness. However, in a therapeutic metaphor for coaching purposes you tend to NOT do that. Just tell the story and let the listener's unconscious mind come up with its own interpretation of what it means.

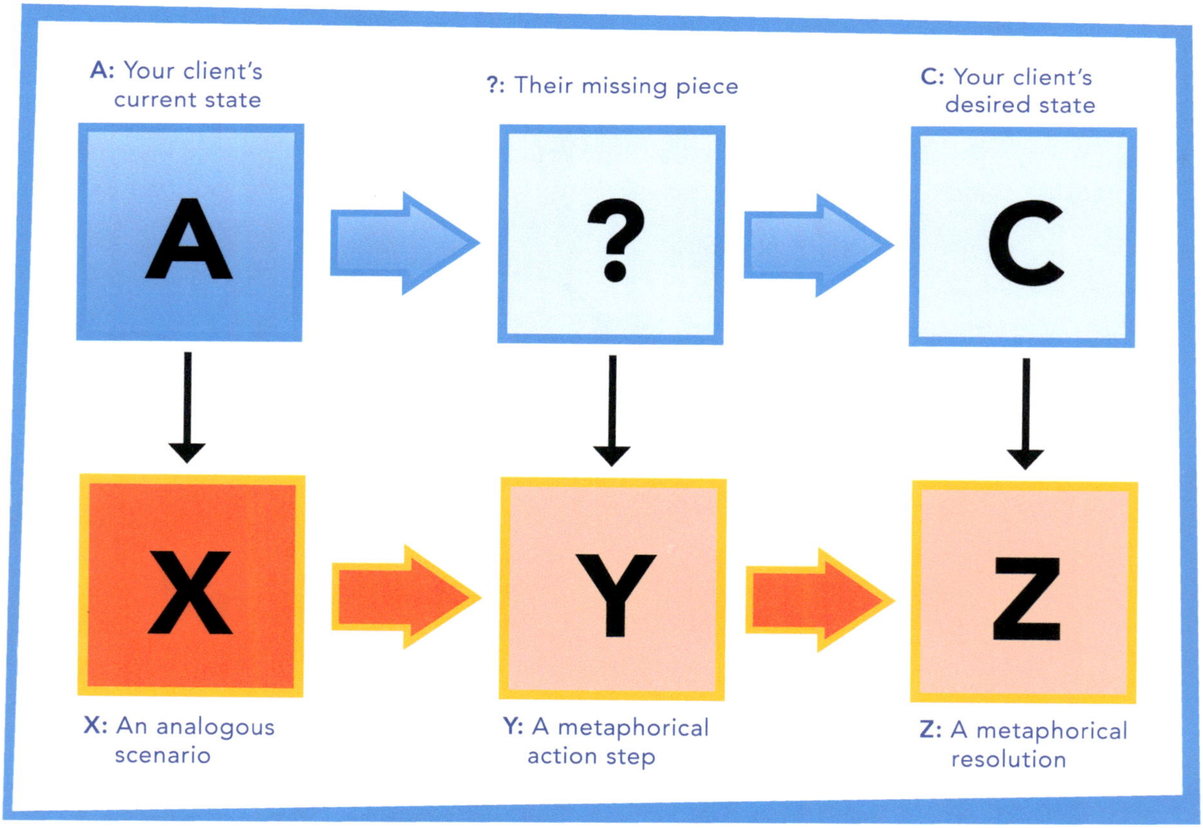

A: Your client's current state

?: Their missing piece

C: Your client's desired state

X: An analogous scenario

Y: A metaphorical action step

Z: A metaphorical resolution

Places to Tell Your Story

" Good stories surprise us. They make us think and feel. They stick in our minds and help us remember ideas and concepts in a way that a PowerPoint crammed with bar graphs never can. "

—Joe Lazauskas and Shane Snow

Places to tell your story

 ## International

The Moth
When & Where: Regular shows in over 50 cities in the United States,
as well as the UK and Australia.
Intensity: The Moth hosts 6 different types of storytelling gatherings of
varying sizes and intensities from casual performance to storytelling competitions.
Event info: themoth.org/events

 ## The United States

The Moth
(see International)

National Storytelling Festival
When & Where: Every fall in Jonesborough, Tennessee.
More info: www.storytellingcenter.net/festival/

Storytelling Live!
When: 2 p.m. Tuesday–Saturday, May through October.
Where: The International Storytelling Center in Jonesborough, Tennessee.
Schedule: www.storytellingcenter.net/storytelling-live/schedule/
Workshops: www.storytellingcenter.net/storytelling-live/workshops/
Applications to perform: www.storytellingcenter.net/storytelling-live/get-involved/

Risk!
When & Where: Risk! tours every month, mostly in the U.S. Stories are also
regularly released on their podcast.
Show times: www.risk-show.com/tour/
Pitch a story: www.risk-show.com/submissions/

Snap Judgment
When & Where: Snap Judgment regularly tours around the contiguous U.S.
Homepage: https://snapjudgment.org
Pitch a story: https://snapjudgment.org/pitches

StoryCorps

When & Where: StoryCorps provides recording locations for you and a loved one to record a story; one person acting as the interviewer and the other acting as storyteller. Recording locations in multiple states, with occasional touring mobile studios.
Listen: https://storycorps.org/stories/
Participate: https://storycorps.org/participate/

The Storytellers Project

When & Where: Regular events are hosted in 20 cities across the US.
Show times: https://www.storytellersproject.com/watch/
Participate: https://storytellersbrandstudio.com/contact

Mortified - Stories from Childhood

When & Where: Regular shows in multiple US cities, and sometimes abroad.
Show times: http://getmortified.com/live/
Participate: http://getmortified.com/participate/

Canada

The Moth

(see International)

(un)told

When & Where: Monthly shows in Ottawa.
Show info: https://www.ottawastorytellers.ca/untold
Participate: https://www.ottawastorytellers.ca/tell-your-stories

Toronto Storytent

When: Every Saturday.
More info: https://storytellingtoronto.org

Vancouver Story Slam

When: The second Tuesday of every month, 8 p.m.
Where: Cottage Bistro, 4470 Main, Vancouver, B.C.
More info: https://www.facebook.com/VancouverStorySlam/

United Kingdom

The Moth
(see International)

Society for Storytelling: National Storytelling Week
When & Where: The first week of February every year
More information: https://www.sfs.org.uk/national-storytelling-week

Natural Born Storytellers
When & Where: Regular events in London
More information: https://www.naturalbornstorytellers.com

15th Century engraving depicting the personification of eloquence

Credits and Sources

" When I was ten, I read fairy tales in secret and would have been ashamed if I had been found doing so. Now that I am fifty, I read them openly. When I became a man I put away childish things, including the fear of childishness and the desire to be very grown up. **"**

—C.S. Lewis

Picture Credits

Frontmatter

8. *Moroccan Storyteller*, Ek Noerg, CC BY-SA 3.0 via Wikimedia commons

Chapter 1

12. Illustration by Gene Sweeney; 15. Father and child vector created by storyset, freepik. com; 16. Illustration by Gene Sweeney; 17. KPDMedia/Shutterstock.com

Chapter 2

18. *The Grandfather Tells a Story*, by Albert Anker, public domain; 21. (top) Released into public domain, (bottom) illustrations by Gene Sweeney; 22. illustration by Gene Sweeney; 23. (photo) A Wolof xalamkat - Dakar, Senegal, public domain, via Wikimedia Commons; kente pattern by Gene Sweeney; 24. Unidentified engraver, public domain, via Wikimedia Commons; 25. British Museum, public domain, via Wikimedia Commons; 26. Trailer screenshot, from DVD *The Ten Commandments*, 50th Anniversary Collection Paramount, 2006, public domain, via Wikimedia Commons; 27. Stained glass: Alfred Handel, d. 1946[1], photo: Toby Hudson, CC BY-SA 3.0, via Wikimedia Commons; 28. (drawing) René Bull, public domain, via Wikimedia Commons, (pattern) by Gene Sweeney; 29. (top) Charles Le Brun, public domain, via Wikimedia Commons, (bottom) Jennie Harbour, public domain, via Wikimedia Commons; 30. Ludwig Emil Grimm, public domain, via Wikimedia Commons; 31. Franz Hanfstaengl, public domain, via Wikimedia Commons; 32. A.F. Bradley, New York, public domain, via Wikimedia Commons; 33. Author unknown, public domain, via Wikimedia Commons

Chapter 3

34. *Ancient Storyteller*, by Amrita Sher-Gil, public domain; 37. The photo is supplied courtesy of the Milton H. Erickson Foundation, all rights reserved; 38. US Postal Service Artwork by C. Robert Moore & Paul E. Wenzel. Moore designed the stamp and Wenzel painted the portrait, public domain, via Wikimedia Commons; 39. National Archives and Records Administration, Public domain, via Wikimedia Commons; 40. Image by OsloMetX from Pixabay; 41. (Ingmar Bergman) Louis Huch (1896-1961), at SF 1930-60, public domain, via Wikimedia Commons; (Frank Capra) NYWT&S staff photographer, public domain, via Wikimedia Commons; (Charlie Chaplin) P.D Jankens, public domain, via Wikimedia commons; 42. (Claire Denis) Elena Ternovaja, CC BY-SA 3.0, via Wikimedia Commons; (Nora Ephron) David Shankbone, CC BY 3.0, via Wikimedia Commons; (Federico Fellini) Walter Albertin, World Telegram staff photographer, public domain, via Wikimedia commons; (Alfred Hitchcock) Ante Brkan, public domain, via Wikimedia Commons; 43. Photo by Roos Trommelen, used with permission; 44. Victor Talking Machine Company (taken by Moss Photo, NYS), public domain, via Wikimedia commons; 46. Illustration by Gene Sweeney; 47. Unknown author, public domain, via wikimedia Commons; 48. Trishhhh, CC BY 2.0, via Wikimedia Commons; 49. Illustration by Gene Sweeney; 50. (Maya Aneglou) Clinton Library, public domain, via Wikimedia Commons; (Pablo Neruda) Biblioteca del Congreso Nacional, CC BY 3.0 CL, via Wikimedia Commons; (Alice Walker) photo by Virginia DeBolt, CC BY-SA 2.0, via Wikimedia

93. Turku Museum Centre, public domain, via Wikimedia commons; 94. Illustration by Gene Sweeney; 96. NBC Television Network, public domain, via Wikimedia commons; 97. photo by Garsya/Shutterstock.com; 98. Ziff-Davis Publishing/Robert Gibson Jones, public domain, via Wikimedia Commons; 99. illustration by Francey/Shutterstock.com; 100. photo by Michelle @Shelly Captures It on Unsplash; 101. photo by Ermolaev Alexander/ Shutterstock.com; 102. photo by Ruslan Zh on Unsplash; 103. Jacques Clement Wagrez, Public domain, via Wikimedia Commons

Chapter 8

104. Illustration by Gene Sweeney; 107. Photo by Halfpoint/Shutterstock.com; 109. Image by Andrew Martin from Pixabay; 111. Illustration by Gene Sweeney

Chapter 9

115. Photo by Kues/Shutterstock.com; 116. Illustrations by Gene Sweeney; 117. Photos by gualtiero boffi/Shutterstock. com; 118. Designed by macrovector/freepik; 119. Scanned by de: Benutzer:Summi, public domain, via Wikimedia Commons; 120. Leonardo da Vinci, public domain, via Wikimedia Commons; 123. drawing by anonymous

Chapter 10

124. Illustration by Gene Sweeney; 127. Classical Numismatic Group, Inc. http://www.cngcoins.com, CC BY- SA 2.5, via Wikimedia commons; 128. Designed by brgfx / Freepik; 130. Photo by Thomas William on Unsplash; 131. Photo by rawpixel on Unsplash; 132. Photo by Yan Krukau from Pexels; 133. Joseph Jacobs, public domain, via Wikimedia Commons; 135. Illustration by Cory Thoman/Shutterstock.com; 137. Photo by David Iliff. License: CC BY-SA 3.0, via Wikimedia Commons; 138. Catabwa County Library, public domain, via Wikimedia Commons; 140. Adapted from a photo by cassidy muir from Pexels; 141. Photo by Jopwell from Pexels

Chapter 11

145. (top) Photo by Ylanite Koppens from Pexels; 145-147. John Mitchell, digital version, Library of Congress, Geography and Map Division, public domain, via Wikimedia Commons; 148. Unknown engraver of the late 15th century, probably in Ferrera, Italy. Public domain, via Wikimedia commons

155. Photo courtesy of the author

Acknowledgements

This book, like all books, is the result of some very wonderful contributions by a number of very wonderful people.

One is Nick Kemp, aka musician Nick Cody, whose idea it was for him and me to take our mutual interest in storytelling and to teach a storytelling seminar together called "Stories from the Outside Inn." He got it all started. Were it not for Nick, this book would never even have been thought of.

Another is Gene Sweeney, the book designer, whose engaging visual imagery and great skill at book layout and design is at *least* half of what makes this book so inviting. I might have written it without Gene, but you probably wouldn't be reading it without Gene's making it magical.

David Gordon's early guidance helped shape this book and his teaching of storytelling, particularly Ericksonian-style therapeutic metaphors, is represented in the Applications section of this book under "Telling Stories in Coaching." Look for his great book *Therapeutic Metaphor: Helping Others Through the Looking Glass*.

Seth Barrish and Josh Broder both generously shared their time and their wisdom with me and made huge contributions, not only to the book, but my whole approach to storytelling. I can't thank them enough.

The same deep gratitude goes to three storytelling teachers I've learned so much from: Matthew Dicks (who also contributed the foreword to this book), Adam Wade and Brad Lawrence. Great storytellers *and* great teachers.

Finally, this book is in your hands thanks to Jennifer S. Wilkov and her team at Your Book Is Your Hook! without whom I couldn't have brought it to life and to wherever you purchased it. I am grateful for her guidance throughout each step of the process to prepare and polish it, put the finishing touches on it, and her support with the publishing and distribution process for it.

I am endlessly grateful to all of these amazing people and to all who have contributed.

Photo courtesy of the Author

ABOUT THE AUTHOR

Doug O'Brien is an award-winning storyteller, story coach, and seminar leader. He teaches classes in Storytelling, Sleight of Mouth, NLP, Ericksonian Hypnosis, and The Havening Techniques®. His podcast, "The Essential Coaching Skills Podcast," is popular weekly listening for many people and his first book, *The User's Guide to Sleight of Mouth,* has been called, "MUCH better than I thought it would be." If you google him he is *not* the hockey player.

ABOUT THE ILLUSTRATOR

Gene Sweeney is a New York City-based designer and illustrator. He enjoys being in a profession where he is able to draw silly pictures and call it productive work. In his spare time, he draws even *sillier* pictures.

A Special Invitation

An exclusive offer to *you* for buying this book . . .

A complete online class on
Storytelling

Discover how to find stories worth telling, craft them into something special,

and then tell them in a way that captivates your audience.

a $497 value

Absolutely FREE as our gift to you.

Yes! A complete, six-part class on storytelling taught by the author.

Plus a *free weekly newsletter* with stories and storytelling tips.

Yours free when you go to

https://www.essentialcoachingskills.com/free_story_class

and sign up!